GCSE
Physics

Brian Arnold

First published 1990

*Copyright © 1990
Brian Arnold*

No part of this publication may be reproduced
or transmitted in any form or by any means,
electronically or mechanically, including
photocopying, recording or any information
storage or a retrieval system, without either
the prior permission in writing from the publisher
or a licence, permitting restricted copying,
issued by the Copyright Licensing Agency,
Alfred Place, London WC1E 7DP

British Library Cataloguing in Publication Data
Arnold, Brian, 1950–
Make the grade in GCSE physics.
1. Physics
I. Title
530

ISBN 0 340 49158 2

*Photoset by PanTek Arts, Maidstone.
Printed in Great Britain for
Hodder and Stoughton Educational,
a division of Hodder and Stoughton Ltd,
Mill Road, Dunton Green, Sevenoaks, Kent
by Richard Clay Ltd, Bungay.*

INTRODUCTION

This book provides students with a concise readable account of all the main topics in GCSE Physics. It will also be of use to those studying balanced science courses, such as Co-ordinated Science, Modular Science or Integrated Science.

The new GCSE examining boards have introduced science courses which are very relevant to the man in the street. Consequently, the concepts and information in this book are presented in the context of everyday applications and events. Physics is an exciting subject – the more it is understood, the more interesting and exciting it becomes.

The layout of this book

This book is divided into eight sections. These are Forces and Motion, Density and Pressure, Work, Energy and Power, Kinetic Theory and Heat, Waves, Electricity and Magnetism, Electronics, and Atomic Structure and Radioactivity. Within these sections a varying number of topics are presented as double page spreads. In this form students can easily dip into a topic in order to support their study notes or as part of a revision programme. For this reason there are GCSE styled questions at the end of each section, which can be used to reinforce understanding or to polish up exam technique. Full answers to all these questions are given at the back of the book.

How to revise

There is no one method of revising which works for everyone. Therefore it is important to discover the approach that suits you best. The following rules may serve as a general guideline.

1 DON'T leave your revision until the last minute. People who can swot up the night before and still do well in an exam are few and far between.

2 DO plan your revision schedule well before the exam. Once you've done this, stick to it – don't be sidetracked.

3 DO find the conditions in which you can revise most efficiently. Some people think they can revise with the television or radio on, but most cannot.

4 DON'T attempt to do enormous chunks of work. Try working for about 1 hour and then rewarding yourself with a break of 15 to 30 minutes while you have a coffee and relax – then back for another hour's revision.

5 DO make a brief summary of the key ideas and facts as you read through your notes/books, but be sure to concentrate on understanding the ideas rather than just memorising the facts.

6 DO attempt to answer some questions from past papers as you finish revising each topic. At first you may need to refer to your notes, but eventually you should attempt the questions unaided as you will do in the exam.

7 DO use your syllabus as a checklist and mark off each topic as you revise it.

8 DO seek help – it may be simply talking to a friend who is doing the same exam or it may be asking a teacher. Whatever the route, don't give up.

Dos and don'ts of tackling the paper

The examination papers set by the different boards will contain three styles of questions.

1 Multiple choice questions

This type of question is usually done on a special answer form which is then computer-marked. With each question you are given four or five possible answers. Your task is to select the correct one. e.g.

1 Which of the following types of radiation is NOT part of the electromagnetic spectrum?

A Infra-red radiation
B Ultraviolet radiation
C Sound waves
D Radio waves
E Microwaves

The answer form may then have
1 A B C D E
2 A B C D E
3 A B C D E
4 A B C D E etc.

Dos and Don'ts

DO select just one answer for each question – if more than one answer has been selected the question will be marked as wrong.

Introduction v

DO keep an eye on the clock. Some questions you will be able to answer immediately you have finished reading them, others may take several minutes to work out – nevertheless, as a rough guide check that halfway through the examination you are approximately halfway through the paper.

DO eliminate those answers you know to be incorrect and then guess, if need be, from those that remain.

DON'T at the end of the examination leave any multiple choice questions unanswered – if all else fails, guess.

2 Short answer or structured questions

This type of question is usually answered on the exam paper itself, often immediately after the question. This gives little opportunity to waffle or go into unwanted depth – short but concise and complete answers are required. e.g.

The radioactive isotope carbon–14 ($^{14}_{6}C$) often used for carbon dating, has a half-life of 5730 years.

1 What is an isotope?

-- (2 marks)

2 What is meant by a 'half-life of 5730 years'?

-- (2 marks)

3 Draw the atomic structure of a carbon–14 atom

.(2 marks)

DO answer the question set, e.g. if the question says STATE then don't EXPLAIN.

DO give as full an answer as you can in the space provided.

DO show all your working out, e.g. write down equations in symbols before substituting in your values.

DO, before the exam, work out approximately how much time there is per mark on your paper, e.g. if the paper is 1 hour long and there are 120 marks available then 1 minute is equivalent to 2 marks. You can now see clearly how long each question should take.

DON'T panic over time, just be aware if you are on target or not. Better to answer lots of questions partly than fully answer a few.

3 Free response or long questions

This type of question requires an extended answer. You must judge how much or how little is required. A good exam technique is particularly important here if you are to gain the maximum number of marks. e.g.

Describe with the aid of a diagram the operation of a refrigerator. Include in your explanation:

(a) the physical changes that occur to the coolant;
(b) any energy transfer that takes place;
(c) the importance of the cooling fins at the back of the refrigerator.

DO read the question carefully to ensure you know precisely what the question is looking for – incorrect interpretations could mean losing all the marks for this question.

DO sketch a plan of attack before tackling the question properly, e.g. are diagrams going to be useful? equations, experimental accounts etc.?

DO consider the inclusion of one or more labelled diagrams. These can often be worth a thousand words – but don't make them too elaborate.

DO show all your workings out – examiners are not mind-readers.

DO be aware of the clock – because of their length, these questions can cause real problems with time. If 15 marks means approximately 15 minutes try not to wander too far from this target time.

DO read your answer carefully when you have finished to confirm that there are no omissions and that you really have written what you wanted to.

One final word – examiners want you to do well. By setting out your answers in a clear, complete and logical fashion you will help them to help you.

CONTENTS

1 Forces and Motion — 2
1.1 Speed and velocity. 1.2 Acceleration.
1.3 Speed, velocity, and acceleration graphs. 1.4 Equations of motion.
1.5 Forces. 1.6 Vectors. 1.7 Moments and stability.
1.8 Force, mass, and acceleration. 1.9 Questions.

2 Density and Pressure — 24
2.1 Density. 2.2 Pressure. 2.3 Pressure in liquids.
2.4 Pressure in gases. 2.5 Questions.

3 Work, Energy and Power — 32
3.1 Energy. 3.2 Energy conservation and transformation.
3.3 Work and power. 3.4 Questions.

4 Kinetic Theory and Heat — 40
4.1 States of matter. 4.2 Temperature and thermometers
4.3 Thermal expansion and contraction. 4.4 Specific heat capacity.
4.5 Latent heat. 4.6 Evaporation and boiling. 4.7 Gas laws.
4.8 Conduction and convection. 4.9 Radiation.
4.10 Uses of heat transfer. 4.11 Questions.

5 Waves — 72
5.1 Wave properties. 5.2 Sound waves. 5.3 Light: reflection.
5.4 Light: refraction. 5.5 Total internal reflection. 5.6 Lenses.
5.7 Optical instruments. 5.8 The electromagnetic spectrum. 5.9 Questions.

6 Electricity and Magnetism — 102
6.1 Static electricity. 6.2 Electric current.
6.3 Electromotive force and potential difference. 6.4 Resistance.
6.5 Ohm's Law. 6.6 Basic magnetism. 6.7 Electromagnetism.
6.8 Force on a current-carrying conductor in a magnetic field.
6.9 Electromagnetic induction. 6.10 Generators and dynamos.
6.11 The transformer. 6.12 Transmission of electricity.
6.13 Electrical power. 6.14 Electricity in the home. 6.15 Questions.

7 Electronics — 148
7.1 Controlling and using electrons. 7.2 Semiconductors.
7.3 Electronic systems and gates.

8 Atomic Structure and Radioactivity — 158
8.1 The Rutherford–Bohr atom. 8.2 Radioactivity.
8.3 Nuclear power. 8.4 Questions.

Answers — 171

FORCES AND MOTION
1.1 Speed and velocity

Speed

The athlete in this drawing can run 100 m in 10 s. Therefore, on average, he will travel 10 m each second, i.e. his speed is 10 m/s.

To calculate the speed of an object we use the equation

$$\text{speed} = \frac{\text{distance travelled}}{\text{time taken}}$$

Distance travelled = 3000 km
Time taken = $1\frac{1}{2}$ h
Speed = 2000 km/h

Distance travelled = 50 cm
Time taken = 500 s
Speed = 0.1 cm/s

Velocity

In everyday life, we often use the words speed and velocity as if they mean the same. To a scientist, however, there is a difference. The story below might help you to understand this difference.

Two trains were travelling along the same single railway track. One was travelling at 100 km/h and the other at 101 km/h. The two trains collided. Very few of the passengers realised there had been a crash, no one was hurt and both trains travelled on to their final destinations.

On the following day another two trains were travelling at 100 km/h and 101 km/h respectively. This time when the trains collided everyone knew what had happened. Many people were injured and both trains left the track. How can two apparently identical situations give rise to two totally different results?

To solve this problem it is necessary to realise that a vital piece of information has been withheld. To be able to predict the outcome of the collision, it is necessary to know not only the speed of each of the trains, but also their directions. In the first collision both trains were travelling in the same direction. The collision speed was therefore 1 km/h (i.e. 101 km/h − 100 km/h). In the second collision the trains were travelling in opposite directions. The collision speed was 201 km/h (101 km/h + 100 km/h).

If we just say how fast an object is moving, we are stating its **speed**. If, as is needed in the train story, we state how fast an object is moving *and* in which direction, we are stating its **velocity**.

Measurements or quantities which give only one piece of information are called **scalars**. Speed is a scalar. Measurements or quantities which give two pieces of information are called **vectors**. Velocity is a vector. E.g. 40 m/s is a speed but 40 m/s in a northerly direction is a velocity. (see also section 1.6)

FORCES AND MOTION
1.2 Acceleration

When an object increases its velocity, we say that it is **accelerating**. When an object decreases its velocity we say it is **decelerating**.

Many car manufacturers publicise the accelerations of their cars in magazines and newspapers in order to attract customers.

Car A can accelerate from 0 – 100 km/h in 10 s.

Car B can accelerate from 0 – 120 km/h in 30 s.

At the moment it is quite difficult to compare the performance of each of these cars. To make the comparison easier, we should work out by how much each car increases its velocity in just one second. This is the car's acceleration.

The acceleration for car A is 10 km/h per second.
The acceleration for car B is 4 km/h per second.

From the above we can see that the *average* acceleration of an object can be calculated using the equation

$$\text{acceleration} = \frac{\text{change in velocity}}{\text{time taken}}$$

Example

A toy car accelerates from 0.5 m/s to 2.5 m/s in 5 s. Calculate its average acceleration.

$$\text{acceleration} = \frac{\text{change in velocity}}{\text{time taken}}$$

$$= \frac{2.5 \text{ m/s} - 0.5 \text{ m/s}}{5 \text{ s}}$$

$$= 0.4 \text{ m/s per second (more usually written as } 0.4 \text{ m/s}^2)$$

Acceleration due to gravity

One of the commonest ways an object can accelerate is by falling. Objects which fall 'freely' under the gravitational pull of the Earth all experience the same acceleration. The experiment below shows how this acceleration can be determined.

To determine the acceleration due to gravity (g)

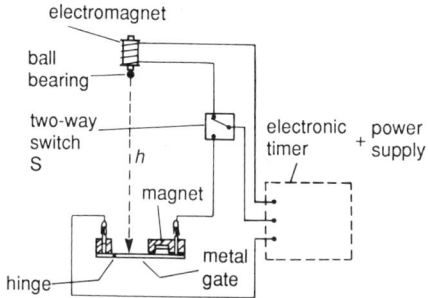

1. Set up the apparatus as shown in the diagram.

2. Open the two-way switch S. When this is done the ball bearing will begin to fall and the electronic timer will start. When the ball bearing strikes the metal gate the timer will stop.

3. Measure accurately the distance the ball bearing falls (h). Note the time taken as indicated on the electronic timer.

4. Reset the apparatus and repeat the experiment several times. Work out an average value for the time (t).

5. Work out a value for g using the equation

$$h = \frac{1}{2} g t^2 \text{ or } g = \frac{2h}{t^2}$$

6. Now repeat the whole experiment with different values of h. The accepted value for g is 9.81 m/s^2.

Q Several seconds after jumping from an aircraft skydivers and parachutists have accelerations which are smaller than g (9.81 m/s^2). Explain why this is so.

FORCES AND MOTION
1.3 Speed, velocity and acceleration graphs

1

In science it is often useful to describe the motion of an object in the form of a graph rather than in words.

Distance/time graphs

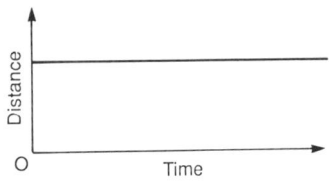

The distance travelled by this object is not changing with time. The object is stationary.

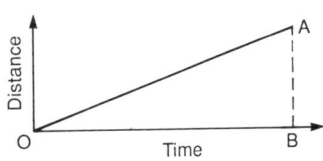

The distance travelled by this object is changing uniformly with time. It is moving at a constant speed.

The size of the speed of the object is equal to the gradient of the graph, i.e. AB/OB.

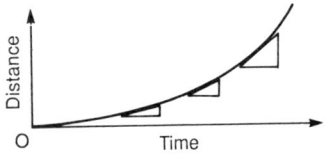

The gradient of this graph is continually increasing. This object is accelerating.

Speed (velocity)/time graphs

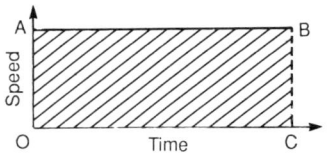

This object is travelling at a constant speed. The total distance it has travelled is equal to the area under the graph (i.e. rectangle ABCO).

Forces and motion 7

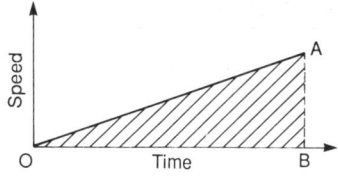

The speed of this object is increasing regularly with time. The object is accelerating uniformly.

The size of the acceleration is equal to the gradient of the graph, i.e. AB/OB.

The distance travelled by the object is equal to the area under the graph i.e. ABO.

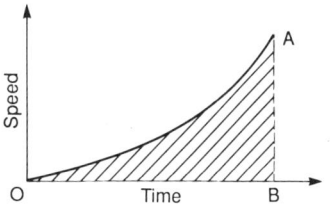

The gradient of this graph is continually changing i.e. the object is not accelerating uniformly. It is accelerating at an increasing rate.

The distance travelled is again equal to the area under the graph (ABO).

Acceleration/time graphs

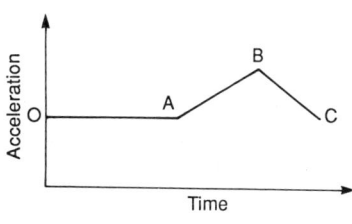

Between O and A the object is accelerating uniformly.

Between A and B the object's acceleration is increasing.

Between B and C the object's acceleration is decreasing.

FORCES AND MOTION
1.4 Equations of motion

Although graphs can be used to solve problems of distance, velocity and acceleration it is often quicker to use equations of motion providing the object moves with uniform acceleration.

The equations are

$$v = u + at$$
$$s = ut + \frac{1}{2}at^2$$
$$v^2 = u^2 + 2as$$

where
u = initial velocity
v = final velocity
a = acceleration
s = distance travelled
t = time taken

Examples

1 Concorde accelerates from rest to 90 m/s in 20 s before taking off.
(a) What is the acceleration of the aircraft and its passengers?
(b) How far down the runway has the aircraft travelled before taking off?

(a) Using
$$v = u + at$$
$$90 \text{ m/s} = 0 \text{ m/s} + a \times 20 \text{ s}$$
$$a = \frac{90 \text{ m/s}}{20 \text{ s}}$$
$$a = 4.5 \text{ m/s}^2$$

(b) Using
$$s = ut + \frac{1}{2}at^2$$
$$s = 0 \times 20 \text{ s} + \frac{1}{2} \times 4.5 \text{ m/s}^2 \times 20^2 \text{ s}^2$$
$$s = 900 \text{ m}$$

Forces and motion

2 An acrobat jumps from a height of 5 m onto a see-saw. What is his velocity as he hits the see-saw? ($g = 10$ m/s^2)

Using
$$v^2 = u^2 + 2as$$
$$v^2 = 0^2 \text{ m}^2/\text{s}^2 + 2 \times 10 \text{m/s}^2 \times 5 \text{ m}$$
$$v^2 = 100 \text{ m}^2/\text{s}^2$$
$$v = 10 \text{m/s}$$

3 A rifle bullet travelling at 200 m/s strikes a wooden beam. If the bullet is brought to rest after travelling 10 cm (0.1 m) into the beam what is its average deceleration?

Using
$$v^2 = u^2 + 2as$$
$$0 \text{ m}^2/\text{s}^2 = 40\,000 \text{ m}^2/\text{s}^2 + 2 \times a \text{ m/s}^2 \times 0.1 \text{ m}$$
$$a = \frac{-40\,000}{0.2} \text{ m/s}^2$$
$$a = -200\,000 \text{ m/s}^2$$

The average deceleration of the bullet is $+200\,000$ m/s^2.

FORCES AND MOTION
1.5 Forces

1

There are many different kinds of force – pushing, pulling, squeezing, twisting, bending, stretching, etc.

On most occasions it is necessary to be in contact with an object in order to apply a force to it.

Sometimes, however, forces can be applied from a distance, e.g. magnetic forces, gravitational forces, electrostatic forces.

In general, if we apply a force to an object it will

(a) change shape   and/or (b) change velocity.

This change in velocity may be because
  (i) the speed of the object increases or
  (ii) the speed of the object decreases or
  (iii) the object changes direction.
How great these effects are depends upon how large the applied force is.

We measure the size of a force in **newtons** (N).

Weight

One of the most important forces we meet in everyday life is the pull of gravity, which we more commonly call **weight**. For example:

The force exerted on an apple by the gravitational pull of the Earth is approximately 1 N i.e. the *weight* of an apple is approximately 1 N.

The force exerted on a 1 kg bag of sugar due to the gravitational pull of the Earth is approximately 10 N.

The weight of a 60 kg woman is approximately 600 N.

On the Moon the gravitational pull is $\frac{1}{6}$ that on the Earth. The weight of the apple, sugar and woman on the Moon would therefore be $\frac{1}{6}$ N, $\frac{10}{6}$ N and 100 N respectively. In deep space, well away from the planets and stars, there are no gravitational forces, i.e. the objects would be **weightless**.

Mass

Although all the objects above weigh less on the Moon than they do on the Earth, they each contain the same amount of matter as before, e.g. there is still 1 kg of sugar in the bag. None of it has disappeared. When we are considering how much there is of an object we are concerned with its **mass**. When we are considering the force we would need to apply in order to lift an object, we are concerned with its **weight**.

We measure the mass of an object in **kilograms** (kg).
We measure the weight of an object in **newtons** (N).

The mass and weight of an object are related by the equation

$$W = m \times g$$

where
W = weight of object (N)
m = mass of object (kg)
g = acceleration due to gravity (9.81 m/s^2 on Earth)

12 *Forces and motion*

Stretching or tensile forces

Stretching forces are very common in everyday life. The extent to which an object stretches often depends on how large a force is applied to it.

A scientist named Robert Hooke carried out many experiments to discover how springs and wires deformed when stretching (tensile) forces were applied to them. His findings are represented in the diagram and graph below.

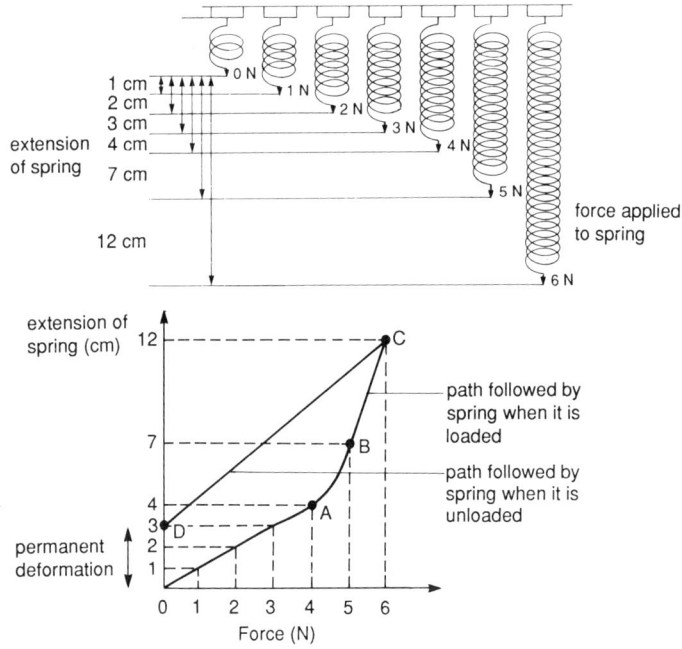

Forces and motion 13

Hooke discovered that, providing the extension was not too great:

> the applied force is proportional to the extension.

This statement became known as **Hooke's Law**.

From the graph on page 12 we can see that Hooke's Law only applies up to point A. This point is known as the **limit of proportionality**.

Up until point B the spring has behaved 'elastically', i.e. if the applied force is removed the spring returns to its original size and shape. Beyond point B (which is known as the **elastic limit**) the spring undergoes 'plastic' deformation and will not return to its original size and shape when the applied forces are removed (CD).

Newton meters

Because springs stretch uniformly when forces are applied to them they are often used to measure the size of a force. E.g. the spring balance or newton meter shown below is measuring the weight of a fish.

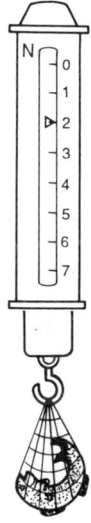

FORCES AND MOTION
1.6 Vectors

In Physics there are many quantities which we measure which have both size and direction. These quantities are called **vectors**. Some examples are displacement, velocity, acceleration, and force.

Quantities which have only one feature, e.g. size, are called **scalars**. Examples are speed, volume, mass, and time.

Scalar quantities can be easily added together. For example if 250 cm^3 of water is added to 125 cm^3 of water, in total there will be 250 + 125 = 375 cm^3.

However, when vectors are added, their direction, as well as their size must be taken into account. For example, a man takes five one-metre paces, stops and then takes another five paces. How far is he from his starting position? At present it is not possible to answer this question unless extra information concerning the directions in which he is walking is given.

Suppose initially the man walks southwards for five paces and then westwards. By drawing a scale diagram to represent his movements we can show that he is now approximately seven paces from his initial starting point in a SW direction as shown below.

Parallelogram of vector addition

The **resultant** of any two vectors can be found using a 'parallelogram of vectors'.

Constructing the parallelogram

1 Draw two lines to represent both the size and direction of the two vectors.
2 Complete the parallelogram of which the vectors form two sides.
3 The diagonal (between the vectors) represents the size and direction of the resultant.

Examples

1. A sailor walks southwards at 3 m/s across a ship which is travelling west at 4 m/s. What is the velocity of the sailor with respect to the sea?

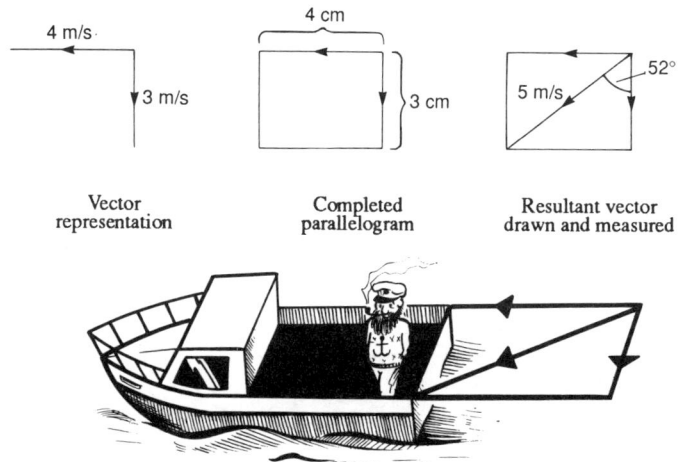

The sailor is walking at 5 m/s in a direction 52°W of S with respect to the sea.

2. What single force is needed to balance these two forces?

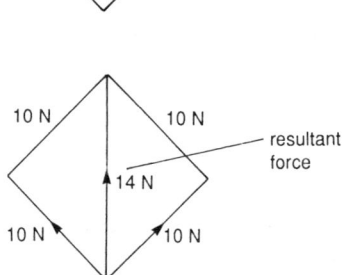

To balance this resultant force an equal and opposite force is needed, i.e. the balancing force needed is 14 N downwards.

FORCES AND MOTION
1.7 Moments and stability

Sometimes when we apply a force, it causes an object to turn or twist, e.g. opening a door or pedalling a bicycle. This turning effect of a force is called a **moment**.
The size of a moment depends upon the size of the force and where it is applied. i.e.

> size of moment = applied force × perpendicular distance of force from fulcrum

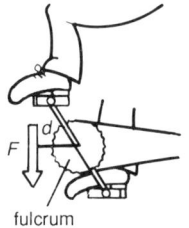

F = applied force
d = perpendicular distance of force from fulcrum

Q Why is it much easier to undo a stiff nut with a long spanner rather than a short one?

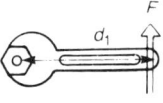

Moment = $F \times d_1$

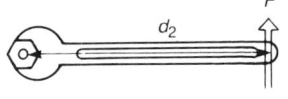

Moment = $F \times d_2$

Balancing moments (principle of moments)

If a pivoted object is balanced the sum of the clockwise moments must be equal to the sum of the anticlockwise moments.

Anticlockwise moment = 1200 N x 1.5 m

= 1800 Nm

Clockwise moment = 500 N x 2 m + 800 N x 1 m

= 1800 Nm

Simple lever

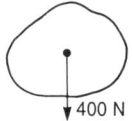 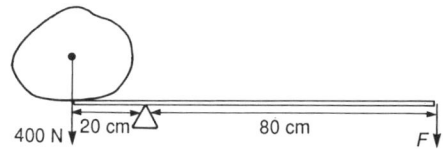

To lift the rock above without using a lever would require a force of 400 N. If, however, a lever is used then by applying the principle of moments we can see the force (F) now needed is much less.

$$400 \text{ N} \times 20 \text{ cm} = 80 \text{ cm} \times F$$
$$\therefore F = 100 \text{N}$$

Wheelbarrow

Moving large amounts of earth around the garden can be hard work. Using a wheelbarrow makes the task much easier.
To lift a load (so that it can be pushed to where it is required) a gardener needs only to create a moment equal to that produced by the soil.
Using the principle of moments to find value of F:

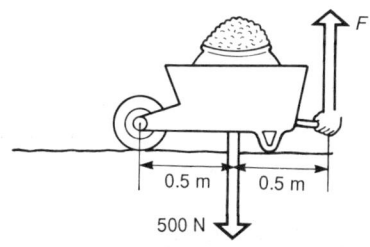

$$500 \text{ N} \times 0.5 \text{ m} = F \times 1.0 \text{ m}$$
$$\therefore F = 250 \text{ N}$$

18 *Forces and motion*

Centre of gravity (mass)

The **centre of gravity** (mass) of an object is that point where we imagine all the weight (mass) of an object to be concentrated. For regular-shaped objects the centre of gravity is often at the geometric centre.

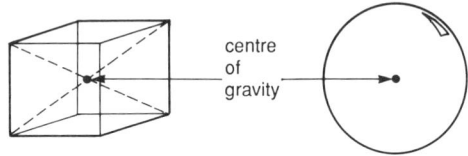

To find the centre of gravity of an irregular-shaped object

1 Hang the object from a pin on a stand so that it is free to swing.
2 Using a plumbline draw a vertical line through the pivot (pin).
3 Hang the object from a different position.
4 Repeat step 2.
5 The centre of gravity is where the two plumblines cross.

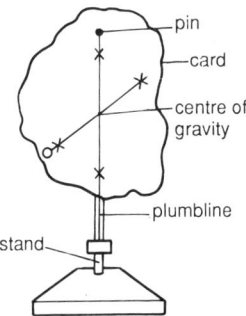

What simple test could we carry out to prove that we had found the centre of gravity of this object?

Stability

When racing cars are designed, a great deal of care and attention is taken to ensure that they are stable, i.e. they are unlikely to turn over. To achieve this, modern racing cars have a very wide wheel base and a low centre of gravity. Consequently, should the car tip a little, its weight creates a moment which returns it to its original position (see the diagram on page 19).

Forces and motion 19

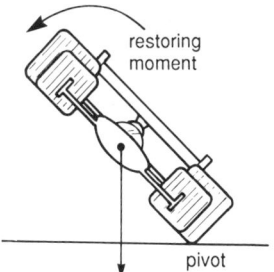

Older racing cars were not so well designed. Their wheel bases are much narrower and their centre of gravity much higher. Consequently when they tilt a little, there is a real danger that their weight creates a moment which causes them to topple over.

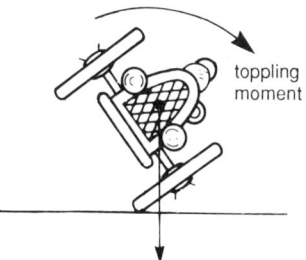

Q Some stunt drivers are so skilled that they are able to drive their cars on just two wheels. Where must the centre of gravity of these cars be when they are being driven?

This object has neutral stability. When tilted it neither falls over nor returns to its original position.

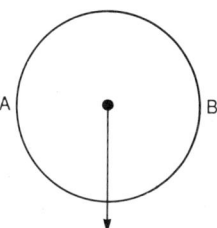
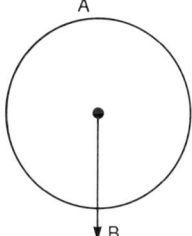

FORCES AND MOTION
1.8 Force, mass and acceleration

Mass and inertia

Wearing seat belts saves lives.

If a car suddenly stops or slows down everything within the car, including its passengers, tries to continue to move. If seat belts are being worn they force the driver and his passengers to change velocity, i.e. decelerate with the car. Without them they are likely to continue moving forward and so collide with the windscreen or dashboard.

Passengers standing up in a bus often experience the opposite problem. As the bus accelerates they feel unable to keep up with it.

In both of these situations there is a reluctance of the body to change its velocity. All objects have this reluctance. It is called **inertia**. The greater the mass of an object, the greater its inertia.

Big rollers like those used on cricket pitches have a large mass and therefore a large inertia – it is difficult to start them moving – and to get them to stop!

Accelerating forces

To overcome inertia, i.e. change an object's velocity, we must apply a force.

In drag car racing competitors try to travel a distance of $\frac{1}{4}$ mile in as short a time as possible – starting from rest. To do this the cars must be capable of high acceleration. They are therefore designed (a) to have as small a mass (inertia) as possible and (b) to have an engine which develops as large a propulsive force as possible.

Forces and motion

To determine the relationship between force (F), mass (m) and acceleration (a).

1. A constant force F is applied to a trolley of mass m.
2. The acceleration of the trolley is measured.
3. Steps 1 and 2 are repeated with different values of F and m.

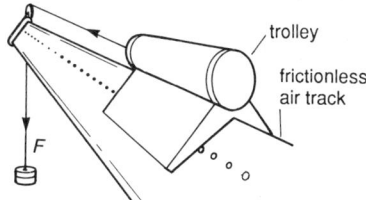

From the results of this experiment we discover that the relationship between F, m and a is

$$F = m \times a$$

Example

A car of mass 500 kg accelerates at 3 m/s². What driving force is being developed by the engine?

$$\begin{aligned} F &= m \times a \\ &= 500 \text{ kg} \times 3 \text{ m/s}^2 \\ &= \underline{\underline{1500 \text{ N}}} \end{aligned}$$

Balanced forces

Forces don't always make objects accelerate, even those objects that are free to move.

As a free-fall parachutist jumps from an aircraft he immediately begins to accelerate at 9.81 m/s² because of the Earth's gravitational pull. However, as his speed increases so does his air resistance and his resultant accelerating force gradually decreases. Eventually the frictional forces and the gravitational pull become equal. There is therefore no resultant force and the parachutist falls at a constant velocity. This is known as his **terminal velocity**.

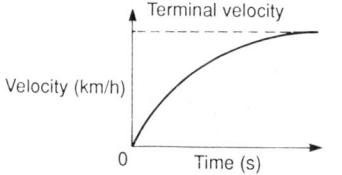

Velocity of parachutist against time

FORCES AND MOTION
1.9 Questions

1 A sprint cyclist travels 500 m in 20 s. What is his average speed?

2 An Intercity train travels at an average speed of 160 km/h. How long will it take to travel 800 km?

3 A Grand Prix racing car has an average lap speed of 180 km/h. How many laps will it do in $1\frac{1}{2}$ hours if each lap is 4.5 km long?

4 The graph below describes the motion of a bus as it travels from village to village.

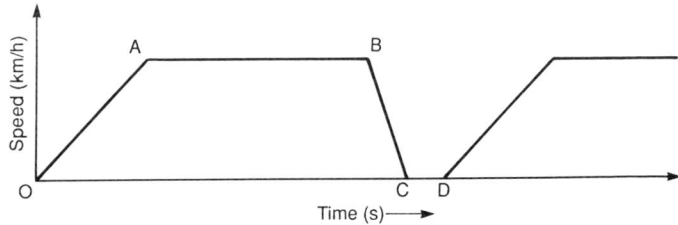

(i) Describe in detail what is happening between OA, AB, BC and CD.
(ii) Sketch an acceleration/time graph for the bus's journey.

5 (i) A car accelerates from 0 to 200 km/h in 20 s. What is the average acceleration of this car? Why is this the *average* acceleration ?
(ii) A train slows down from 120 km/h to 40 km/h in 20 s. What is the deceleration of the train? What is the acceleration of the train?
(iii) A small rocket on bonfire night accelerates from rest to 40 m/s in 4 s. What is the acceleration of the rocket?

6 A stone is thrown vertically upwards. It climbs for 4 s before it begins to fall. ($g = 10$ m/s^2)
(i) What is the speed of the stone at its maximum height?
(ii) What was the initial speed of the stone when it was thrown?
(iii) What is the maximum height the stone reaches?
(iv) For how long is the stone in the air?

Forces and motion 23

7 A ski jumper accelerates down a slope at 5 m/s². If the ski ramp is 90 m long what is his take-off speed? State any assumption you have made. If the jumper flies through the air for 3 s how far from his take-off point will he travel, assuming his horizontal velocity remains constant?

8 What is the final velocity of a car which when travelling at 20 m/s accelerates at 5 m/s² for 8 s?

9 State four possible effects of applying a force to an object. Give an everyday example of each.

10 A pupil carried out an experiment to prove Hooke's Law. Her results are shown in the table below.

Extension (mm)	0.3	0.6	0.9	1.2	1.7
Force (N)	1	2	3	4	5

(i) Draw a graph of the pupil's results.
(ii) Does the graph confirm Hooke's Law? Explain your answer.
(iii) What is likely to happen to this spring when the applied forces are removed?

11 (i) An astronaut of mass 100 kg moves away from his spacecraft by using a small propulsive unit attached to his back. If the maximum force generated by the unit is 20 N what is the maximum acceleration he can achieve?
(ii) The strings of a catapult exert a total force of 2 N on a stone, causing it to accelerate at the rate of 10 m/s². Calculate the mass of the stone.
(iii) A rocket of mass 100 000 kg experiences an acceleration of 2 m/s². Calculate the force being developed by the rocket motors.

12 A pilot flies his aircraft due south at 100 m/s. There is, however, an easterly wind of 10 m/s. What is the true velocity of the aircraft?

DENSITY AND PRESSURE
2.1 Density

2

Everyone knows that steel is heavier than wood and yet a tree is heavier than a nail!

What this statement is trying to say is that a piece of steel is heavier than an *equal volume* of wood. When we are comparing the 'heaviness' of different materials we are really comparing **densities**.

$$\text{density} = \frac{\text{mass}}{\text{volume}}$$

Density is measured in **kg/m³**.

Example

A solid of mass 2 kg has a volume of 0.005 m³. What is its density?

$$\text{density} = \frac{\text{mass}}{\text{volume}}$$

$$= \frac{2\,\text{kg}}{0.005\,\text{m}^3}$$

$$= \underline{\underline{400\,\text{kg/m}^3}}$$

To find the density of regular-shaped objects

1 Weigh the object to find its mass.
2 Measure the object's dimensions and calculate its volume using the appropriate formula.

volume = $l \times b \times h$ volume = $\frac{4}{3}\pi r^3$

3 Calculate the object's density using density = mass/volume.

To find the density of irregular-shaped objects

1 Fill the eureka can with water.
2 Lower the object until it is fully immersed and collect the water which overflows.
3 Measure the volume of the displaced water using a measuring cylinder (this is also the volume of the object).
4 Dry and weigh the object to find its mass.
5 Calculate the density of the object using density = mass/volume.

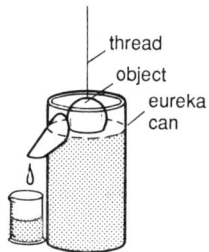

To find the density of a liquid

1 Weigh an empty measuring cylinder (m_1).
2 Pour the liquid into the measuring cylinder – note its volume (V).
3 Weigh the liquid and measuring cylinder (m_2).
4 Calculate the density of the object using

$$\text{density} = \frac{\text{mass}}{\text{volume}} = \frac{m_2 - m_1}{V}$$

To find the density of a gas (air)

1 Find the mass of the flask while it contains air (m_1).
2 Using a vacuum pump remove the air from the flask.
3 Find the mass of the evacuated flask (m_2).
4 Fill the flask with water.
5 Determine the volume of the flask by using a measuring cylinder to find the volume of water (V).
6 Calculate the density of the air using

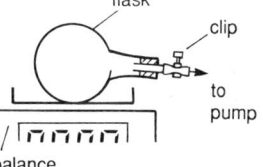

$$\text{density} = \frac{\text{mass}}{\text{volume}} = \frac{m_1 - m_2}{V}$$

Typical densities

Air	1.29 kg/m^3	Water	1000 kg/m^3
Mercury	13 600 kg/m^3	Ice	920 kg/m^3
Cork	240 kg/m^3		

DENSITY AND PRESSURE
2.2 Pressure

2

If we apply a force to an object, its effect often depends upon how it is concentrated.

The two Eskimos above are both the same weight. The Eskimo on the left, however, is wearing snow shoes. His weight, therefore, is spread over a larger area than that of his friend. Consequently, although his friend sinks into the snow, he does not.

When we are concerned with the distribution or concentration of a force we are dealing with **pressure** (*p*).

$$\text{pressure} = \frac{\text{force}}{\text{area}}$$

We measure pressure in **pascals** where 1 **pascal** (Pa) = 1 N/m².

The pressure exerted by this box depends upon the face on which it stands.

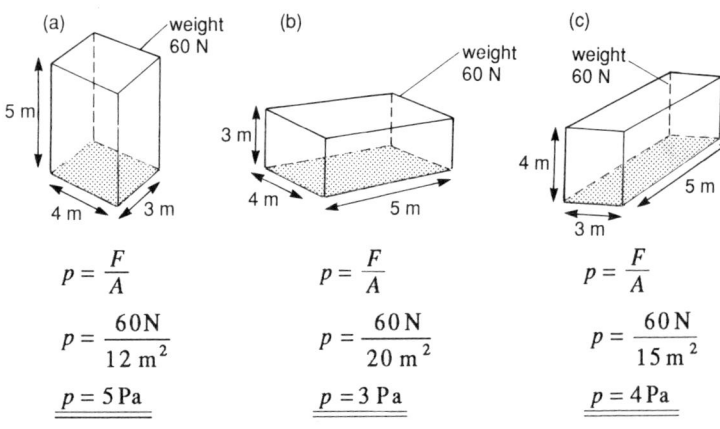

(a)
$p = \dfrac{F}{A}$

$p = \dfrac{60\,\text{N}}{12\,\text{m}^2}$

$\underline{\underline{p = 5\,\text{Pa}}}$

(b)
$p = \dfrac{F}{A}$

$p = \dfrac{60\,\text{N}}{20\,\text{m}^2}$

$\underline{\underline{p = 3\,\text{Pa}}}$

(c)
$p = \dfrac{F}{A}$

$p = \dfrac{60\,\text{N}}{15\,\text{m}^2}$

$\underline{\underline{p = 4\,\text{Pa}}}$

DENSITY AND PRESSURE
2.3 Pressure in liquids

This diver is experiencing pressure which is being exerted by the liquid around him. The size of the pressure is determined by the weight of the water (liquid) directly above him and can be calculated using the formula

$$p = h \times \rho \times g$$

where
h = height of liquid
ρ = density of liquid
g = acceleration due to gravity (9.81 m/s^2)

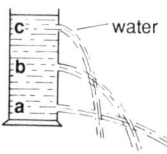

Pressure in a liquid increases with depth
i.e. $p_a > p_b > p_c$

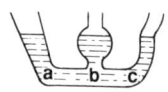

The width or shape of a column of liquid does not affect pressure
i.e. $p_a = p_b = p_c$

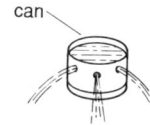

Pressure in a liquid is the same in all directions

Hydraulics

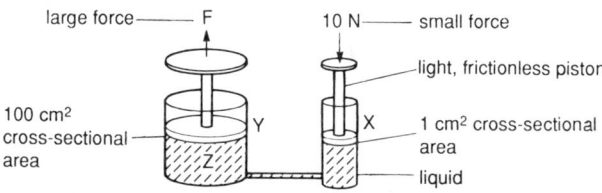

Liquids are incompressible, i.e. they cannot be squashed. If, therefore, a force of 10 N is applied via piston X (as shown above) it will create throughout the liquid a pressure of 10 N/cm^2.

At Z the pressure in the liquid must still be 10 N/cm^2. If, therefore, the cross-sectional area of piston Y is 100 times bigger than that of piston X, F must also be 100 times bigger ($F = p \times A$), i.e. 1000 N. So a small force applied at X has resulted in a much larger force being applied at Y. This is the principle behind the hydraulic jack.

DENSITY AND PRESSURE
2.4 Pressure in gases

Demonstrating the effects of atmospheric pressure

When the air is withdrawn from this can there is no internal pressure to balance the atmospheric pressure. The can therefore collapses.

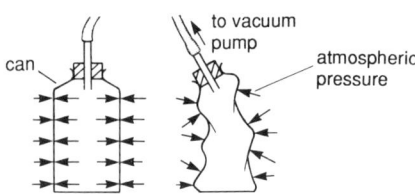

When the sucker is pushed onto the wall the air inside is squeezed out. When released, the sucker is held against the wall by atmospheric pressure.

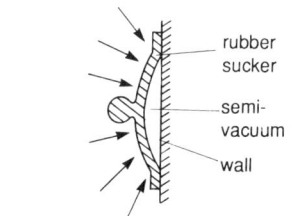

When the air in this straw is sucked out atmospheric pressure pushes the liquid upwards.

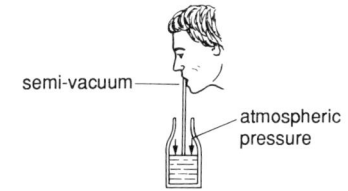

When a full bottle of water is inverted as shown, the water is supported by atmospheric pressure.

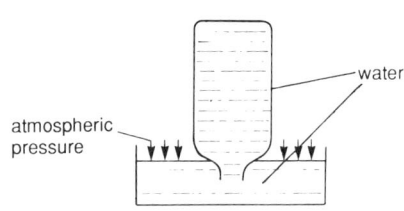

Measuring atmospheric pressure

If the inverted bottle above were replaced by a very long tube sealed at the top, we would discover that there was a maximum height of water the

Density and pressure

atmospheric pressure would support (normally this is approx. 10 m). If the atmospheric pressure alters, so too does the height of the column of water it supports. In fact

atmospheric pressure = $h \times \rho \times g$

where
h = height of column
ρ = density of liquid
g = acceleration due to gravity (9.81 m/s²)

If a much denser liquid, such as mercury, is used, a smaller column will be supported: for mercury this would be approximately 0.76 m high. This apparatus (a mercury barometer) can be used to measure changes of atmospheric pressure.

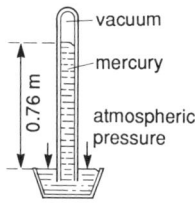

Aneroid barometer

If the atmospheric pressure increases, the box is slightly crushed which causes the pointer to move. When atmospheric pressure decreases, the box expands and the pointer moves the other way. This kind of barometer is not very accurate but is compact and portable.

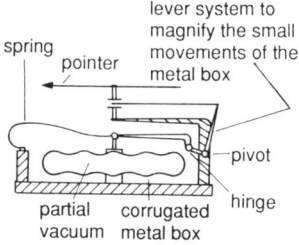

The manometer – measuring the pressure of a gas supply

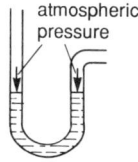

Before the supply is turned on the liquid in both limbs is level.

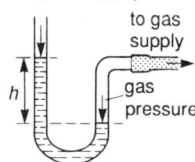

When the supply is turned on the liquid moves to the position shown above. The excess pressure of the supply is given by

$p_{gas} = h \times \rho \times g$

DENSITY AND PRESSURE
2.5 Questions

2

1. Describe how you would find the density of cork using a cork, needle, eureka can, beaker of water, measuring cylinder and balance.

2. Using the information below calculate the density of aluminium, steel and lead.

	Mass (kg)	Volume (m³)	Density (kg/m³)
Aluminium	5	0.0018	
Steel	15	0.0019	
Lead	100	0.0090	

3. Calculate the pressure exerted on the ground by
   (i) a lady weighing 500 N if the total surface area of her stilleto heels in contact with the ground is 0.0025 m².
   (ii) an elephant weighing 5000 N if the total surface area of the soles of his feet is 0.1 m².
   (iii) a man weighing 750 N if the total surface area of his shoes in contact with the ground is 0.125 m².

4. Explain what is likely to happen here.

Density and pressure 31

5 (i) Calculate the extra pressure exerted on a diver swimming at the bottom of a lake 20 m deep.
  (ii) Would the pressure exerted upon him have been greater or smaller had he been diving in sea water? Explain your answer.
  (iii) Whilst at the surface of the lake the diver fills a spherical balloon with air and then takes it to the lake bed below. Explain clearly what happens to the balloon and why.
  (density of water = 1000 kg/m^3, acceleration due to gravity = 9.81 m/s^2)

6 Why do pilots of very high flying aircraft wear pressurised suits?

7 Describe how you would use a manometer to compare the lung pressures of a class of pupils.

WORK, ENERGY AND POWER
3.1 Energy

3

Anything which is able to do work is said to possess **energy**. Someone who is energetic is capable of doing a lot of work. We use energy to do something useful for us. Energy is measured in **joules** (J).

Different types of energy

Kinetic energy   is the energy an object possesses because of its motion.

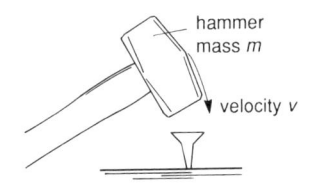

This hammer is able to knock a nail into a piece of wood because it is moving. It has kinetic energy (K.E.) = $\frac{1}{2} mv^2$.

Potential energy is the energy an object possesses because of its position or shape.

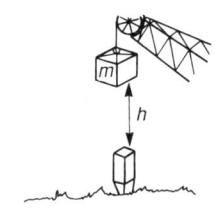

This weight has gravitational potential energy (P.E.) which is being used to drive a pile into the ground. P.E. = mgh.

The wound-up elastic potential energy of the spring is moving the hands of this watch.

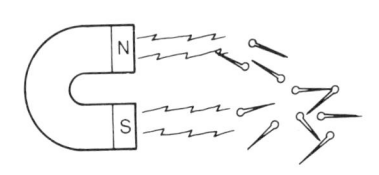

Magnetic potential energy

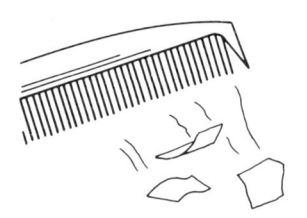

Electrostatic potential energy

Electrical energy is one of the most convenient forms of energy and is the basis of all electrical and electronic appliances. We use it to work radios, hairdryers, washing machines, electric fires, electric trains etc.

Thermal or heat energy All objects at a temperature above zero degrees kelvin are composed of atoms and molecules which are vibrating, i.e. they contain thermal energy. The hotter an object is the greater the movement of the molecules and so the greater the thermal energy.

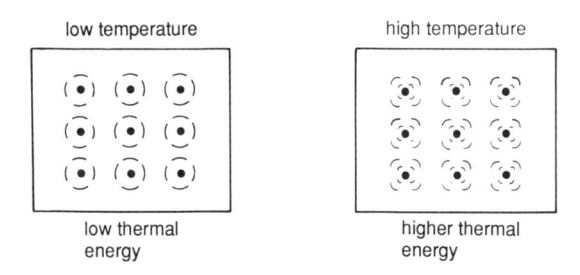

low temperature — low thermal energy

high temperature — higher thermal energy

If two objects at different temperatures are in contact, energy will flow from the hotter to the cooler. This transfer of energy is called **heat** and can be used to drive steam engines and turbines.

Light energy and **sound energy** travel by waves (see p.72) – the energy which we receive from the sun is in the form of light and heat energy.

Chemical energy Sources of chemical energy include oil, gas, coal, and chemical reactions.

Nuclear energy A nuclear submarine obtains all its energy requirements from a nuclear reactor. Nuclear energy, as used in power stations and nuclear-driven submarines, has the potential of being of great benefit to man but unfortunately this energy can be released in a highly destructive manner. A nuclear reactor is described in more detail in chapter 8.

WORK, ENERGY AND POWER
3.2 Energy conservation and transformation   3

When we use energy to do something for us it is never lost. It simply changes into a different form. For example:

Energy in	Device	Energy out
Electrical	Motor	Kinetic
Chemical	Cell (battery)	Electrical
Sound	Microphone	Electrical
Electrical	Light bulb	Heat and light
Chemical	Car	Kinetic and heat
Kinetic	Generator	Electrical
Electrical	Radio	Sound
Potential	Catapult	Kinetic

The energy crisis

Although energy is never lost it frequently ends up in a dilute form which is not very useful. For example, the kinetic energy of a car originates from the fuel it uses. When the car stops, much of this energy is transformed into thermal or heat energy (perhaps in the brakes and their surroundings).

If we continue to use the concentrated forms of energy (such as fossil fuels) at the present rate there is a real danger that there will be an energy shortfall early next century. There are two possible ways in which we could avoid or reduce the effect of this shortfall.

(a) Developing a greater awareness of energy conservation

We could
- increase the efficiency of machines such as cars, aeroplanes, generators etc;
- increase the insulation of houses, offices and factories so that less energy is wasted when these places are heated;
- use objects and materials which can be reused or recycled rather than those that are used once and thrown away, e.g. glass bottles rather than plastic ones.

(b) Making greater use of alternative sources of energy

1 Solar panels These use the energy from the Sun to warm water.

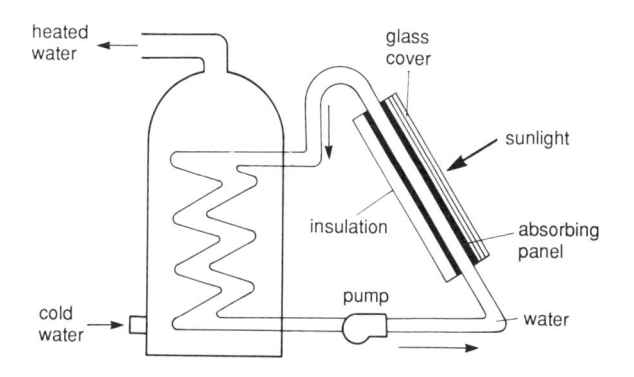

2 Solar cells These convert the Sun's rays into electrical energy. Many modern calculators use solar cells rather than batteries as their energy source.

3 Wind energy After a great deal of research scientists are now building very efficient wind-powered generators which can be used to generate electricity for isolated communities in hilly areas of the country.

4 Tidal energy The waves and the tides of the sea contain vast quantities of energy. As yet, however, they remain untapped as technologists and designers search for an economic way of utilising them.

5 Geothermal energy Deep under ground the temperature of the Earth is very high. By drilling deep shafts where the Earth's crust is thin, or there is a natural fault, it may be possible to tap into this enormous store of energy.

6 Fusion Most of our energy on Earth comes from the Sun. This energy is generated in a nuclear reaction whereby two light elements combine to create a heavier element accompanied by a release of large quantities of energy. At present people are trying to duplicate this reaction here on Earth. If they are successful, it may solve all our energy problems.

WORK, ENERGY AND POWER
3.3 Work and power

In everyday life the word *work* has many meanings but to scientists it is something very precise. Consider the situation described below.

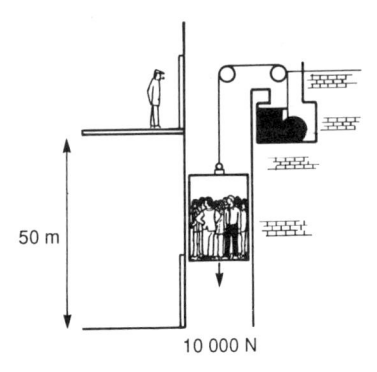

When a lift carries people from the ground floor to one of the upper floors of a hotel the electrical energy needed to power the lift's motors is converted into gravitational potential energy. In doing so the lift has done some work, i.e. *work is done when energy transformations take place.*

An electric light bulb changes electrical energy into heat and light energy, i.e. it is doing work.

A catapult can be used to change elastic potential energy into kinetic energy, i.e. it can do work.

We can calculate the amount of mechanical work done using the equation:

> work done = force × distance moved (in the direction of the force)

Example

If the people in the lift above altogether weigh 10 000 N and the distance they are lifted is 50 m then

$$\begin{aligned}\text{work done} &= \text{force} \times \text{distance moved} \\ &= 10\,000\,\text{N} \times 50\,\text{m} \\ &= \underline{500\,000\,\text{J or } 500\,\text{kJ}}\end{aligned}$$

If a force of 1 N moves through a distance of 1 m, one joule (1 J) of work is done.

Power

Power is the rate at which work is being done. For example the power of an electric fire tells us how quickly electrical energy is being transformed into heat and light energy. The unit of power is therefore joules per second and is more commonly known as the **watt (W)**.

$$\text{power} = \frac{\text{work done}}{\text{time taken}}$$

Examples

If the people in the lift in the diagram on page 36 complete their journey in 25 seconds, what is the power of the lift?

$$\begin{aligned}\text{power} &= \frac{\text{work done}}{\text{time taken}}\\ &= \frac{500\,000\,\text{J}}{25\,\text{s}}\\ &= 20\,000\ \text{W or}\ 20\,\text{kW}\end{aligned}$$

Efficiency

If we measure the electrical energy fed into the lift's motors, we would find it to be much larger than 500 000 J. This is because some of this energy is used (a) to overcome frictional forces, and (b) to raise the lift itself.

If the energy input was 1 000 000 J and the useful work done was still 500 000 J we would describe the lift system as being 50% efficient, i.e.

$$\text{efficiency} = \frac{\text{work output}}{\text{work (energy) input}} \times 100\%$$

WORK, ENERGY AND POWER
3.4 Questions

3

1 Some workers on a building site have set up an electric winch in order to lift a bucket filled with tiles up to the roof. If the bucket and tiles weigh 500 N
   (i) What is the minimum force that must be applied in order to lift the bucket of tiles off the ground?
   (ii) How much work is done in lifting the tiles 20 m from the ground to the roof?
   (iii) What energy transformations are taking place as the tiles are raised?
   (iv) If the tiles are lifted 20 m in 10 s, what is the power of the winch?
   (v) If the winch is only 50% efficient, how much energy must be fed into the electrical motor to lift the tiles the 20 m?
   (vi) Suggest one or two reasons why the system might be less than 100% efficient.
   (vii) How can the efficiency of the system be improved?

2 To be a good pole vaulter it is essential not only to be strong and agile but also to have good sprinting speed.
   (i) What kind of energy does a vaulter possess
      (a) before starting his run?
      (b) as he sprints down the runway?
      (c) as he clears the bar?
   (ii) Assuming the conservation of energy, calculate (approximately) the maximum height he is able to clear if his horizontal velocity as he plants the pole is 9 m/s.
   (iii) The fastest sprinters in the world could probably plant the pole whilst travelling at 10 m/s. What is the maximum height they could clear if they had good pole vaulting technique?
   (iv) Modern pole vaulters can't sprint quite as quickly as 100 m runners and yet the world's best vaulters are clearing heights greater than that calculated in question (iii). Suggest where they gain the extra energy needed to achieve such heights.
   (v) When a competitor has completed his vault where has all the energy gone?

Work, energy and power 39

3 At night time when most of us are asleep the demand for electricity is quite small. The generators at the power stations, however, are still working as it is very wasteful and inefficient to turn them off. In some power stations the excess electrical energy they are manufacturing is used to pump water uphill into dams. Then during the day the water is released and used to drive generators when demand is high.
  (i) What weight of water can be pumped 50 m uphill if the surplus energy from a generator is 2 MJ?
  (ii) When released, how much K.E. will this water have after it has fallen
    (a) 25 m?
    (b) 50 m?
    What assumptions have you made?
  (iii) If the generator driven by the water is only 40% efficient, how much energy is lost?
  (iv) Suggest why off-peak night-time electricity is cheaper than day-time electricity.

KINETIC THEORY AND HEAT
4.1 States of matter

The **kinetic theory** is a series of ideas and models put forward to explain the basic properties of the three states of matter.

Kinetic theory of solids

All solids are made up of tiny particles called atoms or molecules. These are usually arranged in a regular pattern called a **lattice**. Within the lattice are forces of attraction which hold the molecules in place but allow them to vibrate. It is these strong intermolecular attractions which are responsible for the firmness and rigidity of solids.

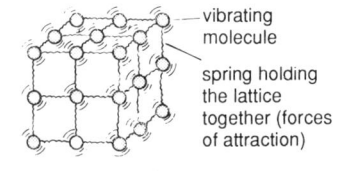

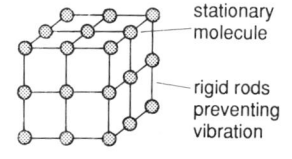

Model of a solid at room temperature — vibrating molecule, spring holding the lattice together (forces of attraction)

Model of a solid at 0 K — stationary molecule, rigid rods preventing vibration

If a solid is cooled, the molecular vibrations decrease until at a temperature of 0 K (–273°C) they stop altogether, i.e. the structure has no kinetic energy.

Evidence to support the kinetic theory of solids

(a) Crystals of a particular substance, e.g. common salt, quartz, are always the same shape. This is because the molecules arrange themselves in a particular lattice structure.

Crystals of common salt

Quartz crystals

(b) It is possible to cleave crystals in certain planes. This is because the cleaving blade is passing between the layers of molecules.

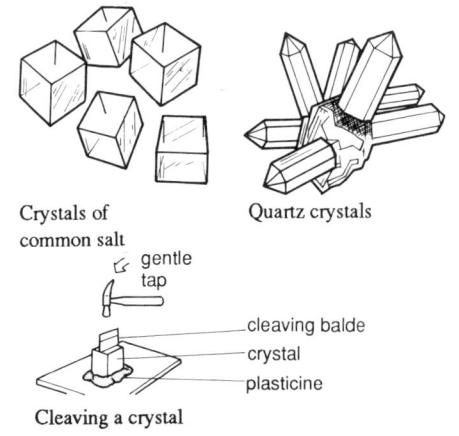

gentle tap
cleaving balde
crystal
plasticine

Cleaving a crystal

Melting

If we heat a solid sufficiently its molecular vibrations become so violent that the lattice structure begins to break down. There is no longer a large regular rigid structure but rather large groups of molecules which are free to move and slide past each other. The solid has **melted**.

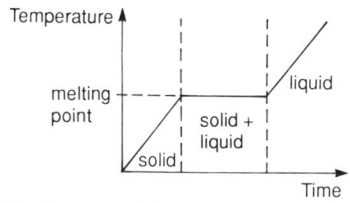

Heating up a solid

The energy which is needed to break down the lattice structure in order to produce a liquid is known as the **latent heat of fusion**. The temperature will remain constant whilst this energy is provided.

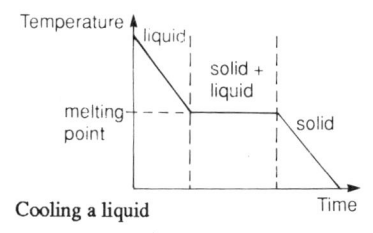

Cooling a liquid

The latent heat is released as the liquid solidifies. This prevents the temperature from falling until all the liquid has become solid.

Kinetic theory of liquids

It is not possible to draw the molecular structure of a liquid as it was for a solid because liquids have no fixed shape. Instead there are large groups of molecules held together by attractive forces which are able to move and slide past each other, i.e. liquids can *flow* and will take the shape of the container into which they are poured.

Evidence to support the kinetic theory of liquids

1 **Diffusion** – If we place a crystal of potassium permanganate in a beaker of water it will gradually dissolve. If the molecules of the water were not moving around, the colour from the dye would remain at the bottom of the beaker – but this is not the case. The colour spreads throughout the water. This suggests that the liquid molecules are sufficiently free to be able to move around. The mixing caused by molecular motion is called diffusion.

2 **Brownian motion** – see kinetic theory of gases.

Boiling

If we heat a liquid sufficiently, its molecular vibrations become so violent that the groups of molecules begin to break down. At this stage the liquid is changing to a gas, i.e. it is **boiling**.

The energy which is needed by the liquid molecules to overcome the attractive forces is known as the **latent heat of vaporisation**.

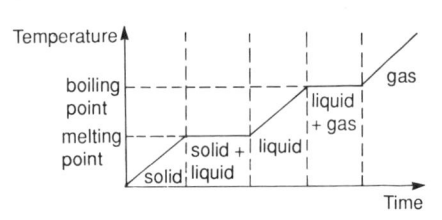

Kinetic theory of gases

The molecules of a gas are completely free and experience no intermolecular forces. Even at room temperature their velocities are very high (approx. 500 m/s). If heated, the molecules will move even faster.

Evidence to support the kinetic theory of gases

1 **Brownian motion** If we observe the motions of smoke particles in air using a microscope we will see that they move about in a random haphazard fashion, as shown in the diagram below. We believe that they do this because they are being jostled by the much smaller but fast-moving molecules of the air. This motion – called Brownian motion – confirms that the molecules of a gas are in continuous random motion.

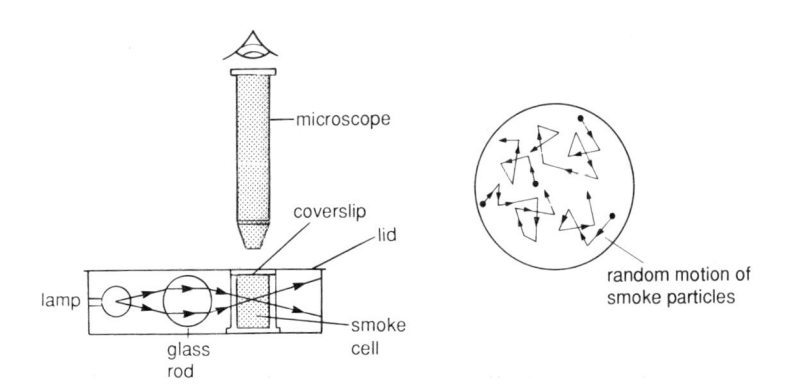

A similar motion can be seen in liquids, using grains of pollen rather than smoke particles. But this movement is much slower than that shown by gases.

2 **Diffusion** After just two to three minutes the molecular motions of the two gases will have caused them to mix or **diffuse**, as shown below.

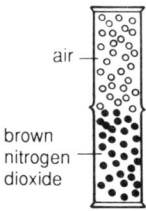

Before diffusion

After diffusion

Summary

	SOLID	LIQUID	GAS
Structure	Regular firm lattice	No fixed structure	No fixed structure
Intermolecular forces	Strong	Quite strong	None
Molecular spacing	Small	Quite small	Very large
Degree of freedom	Low – atoms in fixed positions – can vibrate from side to side	Medium – groups of atoms can move past each other	Completely free
K.E.	Low	Higher than a solid	Higher than a solid or liquid

KINETIC THEORY AND HEAT
4.2 Temperature and thermometers

4

Temperature is a measure of hotness.

Our senses are not very good judges of temperature: although they can give us some idea of how hot an object is, to measure the temperature accurately we use a **thermometer**. One of the most common is the mercury-in-glass thermometer.

Mercury-in-glass thermometer

As the mercury in the bulb of the thermometer becomes warm, it expands and rises up the thin capillary tube. The higher the temperature the further the column rises.

Constructing the scale for a mercury-in-glass thermometer

1 The bulb of the thermometer is placed in pure melting ice and the **lower fixed point** marked.

2 The bulb is now placed in pure boiling water and the **upper fixed point** marked.

3 The distance between these two points is divided into 100 equal divisions. Each division measures a temperature of 1°C on the **Celsius** scale.

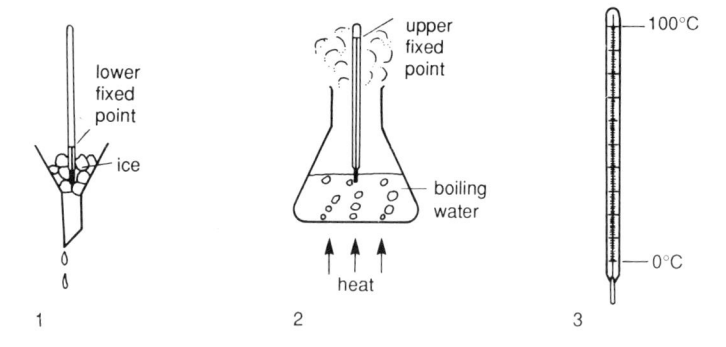

Mercury is used in thermometers because it expands regularly, is easy to see and can be used over a wide range of temperatures (350°C to −40°C). To measure lower temperatures, e.g. in Arctic conditions, an alcohol-in-glass thermometer is often used.

Clinical thermometer

This is a mercury-in-glass thermometer, used primarily to measure body temperature (normally 37°C).

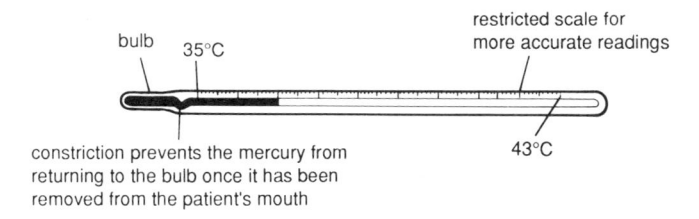

constriction prevents the mercury from returning to the bulb once it has been removed from the patient's mouth

After the temperature has been read the mercury is returned to the bulb by shaking the thermometer.

Other thermometers

Any property which changes regularly with temperature can be used as the basis of a thermometer.

Thermistors and resistance thermometers

The electrical resistance of a **thermistor** (see p.111) changes greatly with temperature. This makes it an ideal device for measuring or detecting temperature change.

The electrical resistance of a piece of wire increases with temperature. We can therefore, by measuring its resistance, determine its temperature. This type of **resistance thermometer** can be used to measure very high temperatures.

Thermocouples

If two wires of dissimilar metals are twisted together at each end and the ends held at different temperatures, an e.m.f. (voltage) is produced. By measuring the size of the e.m.f. we can find the temperature difference between the junctions.

Thermochromic thermometers

This type of thermometer uses colour as a means of indicating temperature.

KINETIC THEORY AND HEAT
4.3 Thermal expansion and contraction

4

When large structures such as bridges are designed, great care must be taken to allow for thermal expansion and contraction.

In warm weather a bridge's atoms and molecules gain energy and so vibrate more vigorously. This increased vibration results in expansion. In cold weather there is less molecular vibration and the bridge contracts. For example, the Firth of Forth railway bridge is approximately 1 m longer in the summer than in the winter.

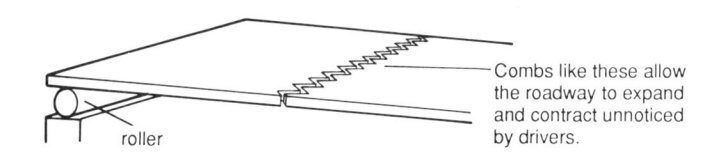

Combs like these allow the roadway to expand and contract unnoticed by drivers.

If this road bridge were fixed at both ends it would buckle or crack as it tried to expand or contract. By supporting the bridge on rollers this movement occurs without damage.

Although, as in the above example, expansion and contraction can be a nuisance, it can also be used to our advantage.

Rivetting

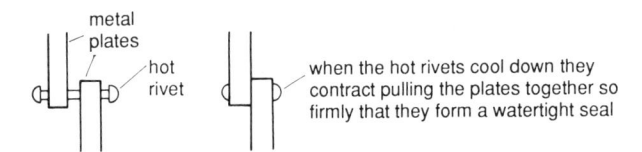

when the hot rivets cool down they contract pulling the plates together so firmly that they form a watertight seal

Q Which building industry makes use of the good seal formed by rivetting?

Shrink fitting

If liquid nitrogen at −196°C is poured over this axle it contracts. A gear wheel can then easily be slipped onto it. As the axle returns to room temperature it expands, resulting in a really tight fit for the gear wheel.

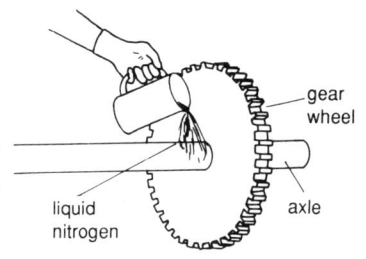

Kinetic theory and heat

Thermostats

When using a steam iron or setting up a tropical fish tank it is important to be able to control temperature. We don't want our expensive clothes being burnt by an iron which is too hot or our tropical fish to die because their water is too cold. To control and keep temperatures constant we use devices called **thermostats**.

At the heart of most thermostats is a bimetallic strip like the one shown below. When heated, the two metals which make up the strip expand by differing amounts. Here aluminium expands more than iron. As a result the strip bends. As it cools the strip returns to its original shape.

(a) Bitmetallic strip when cool

(b) Bitmetallic strip when warm

When an iron, fish tank, etc., reaches the required temperature, its bimetallic strip bends just enough to break the circuit, shown below, and so turns the heater off. As the strip cools it straightens, completes the circuit and so turns the heater back on. This switching on and off of the heater keeps the temperature fairly constant.

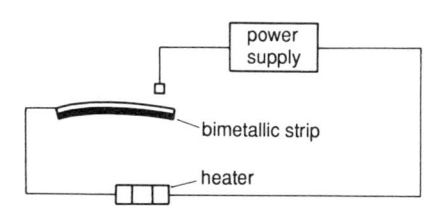

Expansion of liquids and gases

Most liquids when heated expand far more than solids. This is one reason why they are so useful in thermometers (see page 44). Gases, for the same temperature change, usually expand far more than liquids.

KINETIC THEORY AND HEAT
4.4 Specific heat capacity

If we heat an object, the energy it receives usually causes an increase in temperature. The size of the temperature increase depends upon

(a) how much energy is given to the object (H),
(b) how much there is of the object, i.e. its mass (m),
(c) the material from which the object is made, i.e. its specific heat capacity (c).

For example, if we take equal masses of water and oil and give them the same amount of energy, we would find that the oil increases its temperature by nearly twice as much as the water. This is because the water has a bigger appetite for energy, i.e. a bigger **specific heat capacity** (c).

The specific heat capacity of a substance is numerically equal to the energy required to increase the temperature of 1 kg of it by 1 K (or 1°C).

i.e.
$$c = \frac{H}{m \times (T_2 - T_1)}$$

or more usually

$$\boxed{H = m \times c \times (T_2 - T_1)}$$

Example

How much energy is needed to increase the temperature of a 3 kg block of iron from 15°C to 65°C? (Specific heat capacity of iron is 460 J/(kg K)).

Using $H = m \times c \times (T_2 - T_1)$
$= 3 \text{ kg} \times 460 \text{ J/(kg K)} \times 50\,°\text{C}$
$= \underline{\underline{69\,000 \text{ J or } 69 \text{ kJ}}}$

Specific heat capacity and the weather

The considerable difference between the specific heat capacity of sea water (3900 J/(kg K)) and that of land, (approximately 700 J/(kg K)) is a major influence on the world's weather and climate.

Consider two places A and B on the same line of latitude, one in the middle of a large land mass, e.g. Central Asia, and the other on the coast, e.g. on the Mediterranean. In Central Asia in the summer the land warms up quickly because of its low specific heat capacity, temperatures of 40°C or more being not uncommon. In winter the land cools rapidly, resulting in temperatures of −35°C or lower. In Mediterranean regions, because of the influence of the sea, temperatures are far less extreme. In the summer, because of its high specific heat capacity, the sea warms up slowly so moderating the temperature of the land. Similarly, in winter the sea cools down slowly, so preventing land temperatures from dropping quickly.

To determine the specific heat capacity of a solid/liquid

1. Weigh the solid/liquid to find its mass (m).
2. Measure its temperature (T_1).
3. Turn on the electric heater and start the stop clock.
4. When the temperature has risen 10°C (T_2) stop the stopclock and note the time for which the solid/liquid was being heated (t).
5. Turn off the heater.

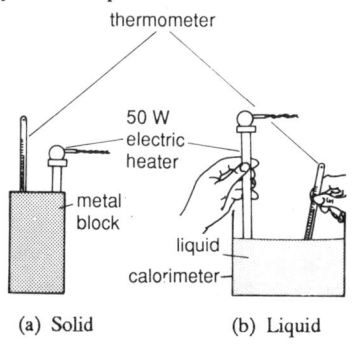

(a) Solid   (b) Liquid

Energy provided by the heater = energy absorbed by the solid/liquid.

$$P \times t = m \times c \times (T_2 - T_1)$$

$$c = \frac{P \times t}{m \times (T_2 - T_1)}$$

In this case $c = \dfrac{50 \text{ W} \times t}{m \times 10°\text{C}}$

KINETIC THEORY AND HEAT
4.5 Latent heat

If we heat some crushed ice taken directly from a freezer, its temperature will rise until its melting point is reached. At this stage the temperature remains steady. This happens because the energy which it is receiving is now being used to melt the ice rather than change its temperature. This energy is known as the **latent heat of fusion.**

Once all the ice has changed to water, the temperature continues to rise until its boiling point is reached. Once again the temperature remains constant. The energy which the water is now receiving is being used to change it into steam. This energy is known as the **latent heat of vaporisation.**

AB – Ice increases in temperature.
BC – Ice melts – no temperature increase.
CD – Water increases in temperature.
DE – Water boils – no temperature increase.

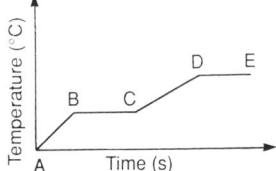

Most solids when heated produce a similarly shaped graph to that shown above for ice.

Specific latent heat (*l*)

The **specific latent heat of fusion** of a substance is numerically equal to the energy required to change 1 kg of the substance from solid to liquid without temperature change.

To determine the specific latent heat of fusion of ice

1. Turn on the heater.
2. When the ice is melting freely, collect the water which drops from the funnel over a period of time (*t*), e.g. 200 s.
3. Weigh the water collected to find its mass (*m*).

If the energy provided by the heater equals the energy taken in by the ice in melting,

$$P \times t = m \times l$$
$$l = \frac{P \times t}{m}$$

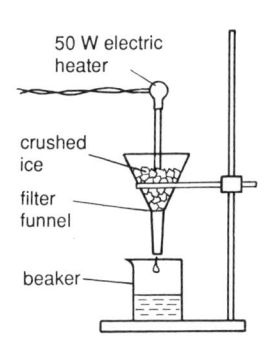

In this case,

$$l = \frac{50 \text{ W} \times 200 \text{ s}}{m}$$

The accepted value of the specific latent heat of fusion of ice is 336 000 J/kg.

The **specific latent heat of vaporisation** of a substance is numerically equal to the quantity of energy required to change 1 kg of the substance from liquid to vapour without temperature change.

To determine the specific latent heat of vaporisation of water

1 Suspend a 3 kW electric kettle from a balance.
2 Turn on the kettle.
3 When the water is boiling freely, note down the mass of the kettle and water (m_1) and start the stopclock.
4 After 300 s again note the mass of the kettle and water (m_2). Turn off the kettle.
5 Work out the mass of the water which has been boiled away ($m_1 - m_2$).

If the energy provided by the heater equals the energy taken in by the water when boiling,

$$P \times t = (m_1 - m_2) l$$
$$\therefore l = \frac{P \times t}{(m_1 - m_2)}$$
$$\text{In this case}, \ l = \frac{3 \times 1000 \text{ W} \times 300 \text{ s}}{(m_1 - m_2) \text{ kg}}$$

The accepted value for the specific latent heat of vaporisation of water is 2 300 000 J/kg.

KINETIC THEORY AND HEAT
4.6 Evaporation and boiling

There are two ways in which a liquid can change into a gas:
(a) by evaporating,
(b) by boiling.

Evaporation

The molecules of a liquid do not all have the same kinetic energy (K.E.). Individual molecules which are moving very quickly may have sufficient energy to escape the intermolecular attractions of their neighbours, break through the surface layer of liquid and become a gas or vapour molecule. This escaping of individual high K.E. liquid molecules is called **evaporation**.

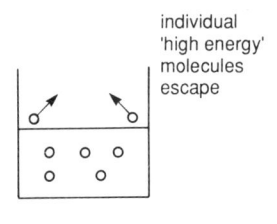

individual 'high energy' molecules escape

Evaporation

Boiling

If the temperature of a liquid is gradually increased, more and more of its molecules gain sufficient energy to escape. Eventually a temperature is reached when the average K.E. of the molecules is high enough for them all to escape. At this temperature the liquid begins to **boil**.

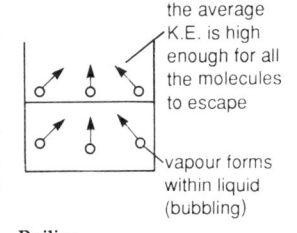

the average K.E. is high enough for all the molecules to escape

vapour forms within liquid (bubbling)

Boiling

Evaporation

Only takes place at the surface of the liquid.
Takes place over a wide range of temperatures.
Rate of evaporation is affected by:
(a) pressure,
(b) surface area of liquid,
(c) movement of air over surface.

Boiling

Takes place throughout the liquid (bubbling).
Takes place at one fixed temperature (at constant pressure).
Rate of boiling is not affected by (b) or (c).

Kinetic theory and heat

Evaporation and cooling

If a large number of high K.E. molecules escape from a liquid, the average K.E. of those remaining will decrease. This results in the temperature of the liquid falling.

Cooling by evaporation is fairly common in everyday life. After climbing out of a swimming pool we may feel cold. This is because the water on our skin is taking energy from us as it evaporates. When we are hot, we perspire; the liquid evaporates and helps us remain cool.

The refrigerator

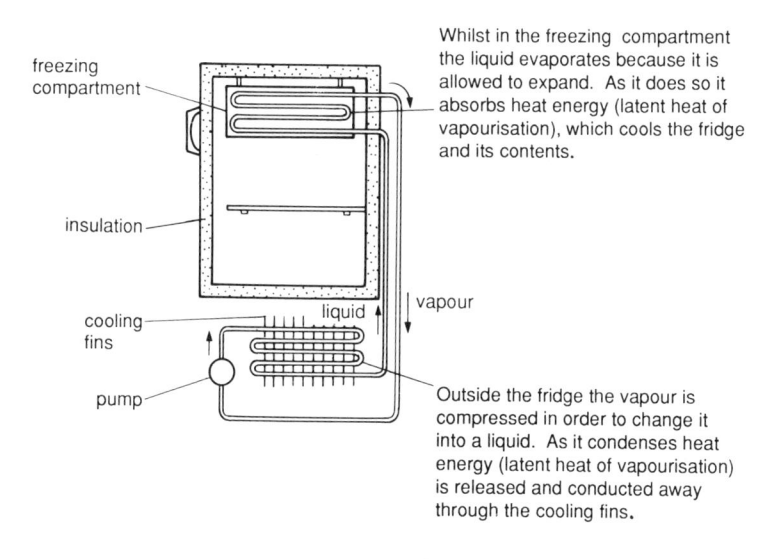

Whilst in the freezing compartment the liquid evaporates because it is allowed to expand. As it does so it absorbs heat energy (latent heat of vapourisation), which cools the fridge and its contents.

Outside the fridge the vapour is compressed in order to change it into a liquid. As it condenses heat energy (latent heat of vapourisation) is released and conducted away through the cooling fins.

KINETIC THEORY AND HEAT
4.7 Gas laws

4

If we heat a solid or a liquid, we would expect it to expand as the temperature increases. With gases this is not necessarily the case. Any change in the volume of a gas depends not only upon its temperature but also upon its pressure.

Boyle's Law

To investigate the relationship between the volume of a gas and its pressure whilst its temperature is kept constant.

1. The volume (V) and pressure (p) of the column of trapped air is noted.
2. Using a footpump, oil is forced into the tube. The new volume and pressure of the trapped air are noted.
3. The experiment is repeated several times. The results are tabulated and a graph of pressure against 1/volume plotted.

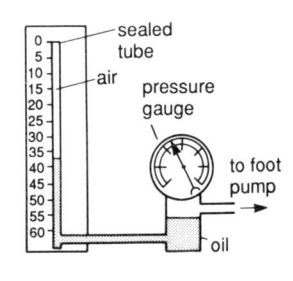

Typical results

Pressure/Pa	Volume/cm³	$p \times V$/Pa cm³
5	60	300
10	30	300
20	15	300
30	10	300

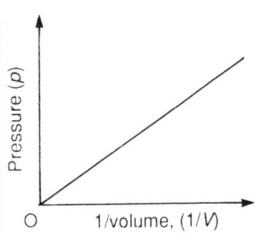

From the table and graph, we can see that
(a) $p \times V$ = a constant and
(b) there is an inverse relationship between p and V, i.e. if we double p we halve V.

These results are summarised by **Boyle's Law:**

> The volume of a fixed mass of gas is inversely proportional to the pressure provided that the temperature remains constant.

Boyle's Law and the Kinetic Theory

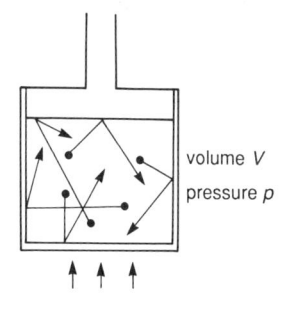

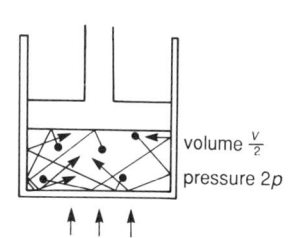

volume V
pressure p

volume $\frac{V}{2}$
pressure $2p$

If the volume which the gas occupies is halved, the rate at which the molecules collide with the sides of the container will double, i.e. the new pressure will be $2 \times p$.

We can express Boyle's Law in the form of an equation:

$$p_1 \times V_1 = p_2 \times V_2$$

Example

A balloon filled with air at a pressure of 10 atmospheres has a volume of 500 m³. If the balloon is now squeezed to $\frac{1}{5}$ of its original volume, what will be the new pressure of the air?

$p_1 = 10 \text{ atm}$ $\qquad$ $p_2 = ?$
$V_1 = 500 \text{ m}^3$ $\qquad$ $V_2 = 100 \text{ m}^3$

Using $p_1 V_1 = p_2 V_2$

$10 \text{ atm} \times 500 \text{ m}^3 = p_2 \times 100 \text{ m}^3$

$\therefore p_2 = \dfrac{10 \text{ atm} \times 500 \text{ m}^3}{100 \text{ m}^3}$

$\therefore p_2 = \underline{\underline{50 \text{ atm}}}$

56 Kinetic theory and heat

Pressure Law

To investigate the relationship between the pressure of a gas and its temperature whilst the volume is kept constant.

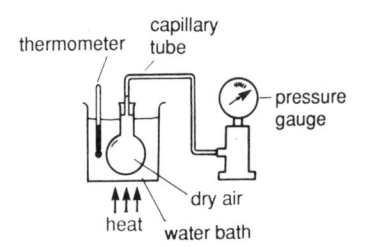

The dry air is heated using the water bath and the temperature of the gas and corresponding changes in pressure are noted.

Typical results

Pressure/Pa	Temperature/°C	Temperature/K	$\dfrac{p/\text{Pa}}{T/\text{K}}$
100 000	27	300	333.3
106 666	47	320	333.3
113 332	67	340	333.3
119 999	87	360	333.3
123 333	97	370	333.3

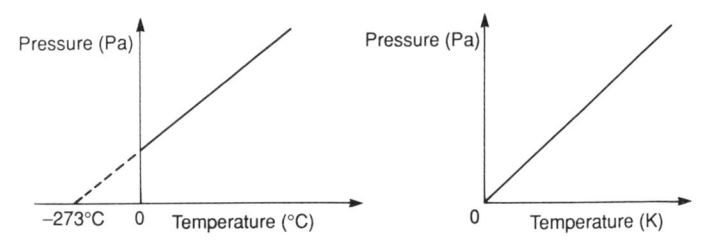

From the table and graphs we can see that
(a) p/T = a constant and
(b) there is a direct proportionality between pressure and temperature providing the temperature is expressed in kelvin.

This relationship between the pressure and temperature of a gas is described by the **Pressure Law** which states:

> The pressure of a fixed mass of gas is directly proportional to its temperature provided that its volume remains constant.

Pressure Law and Kinetic Theory

If the temperature of a gas (expressed in kelvin) is doubled, the rate at which the gas molecules collide with the side of the container will double, i.e. the pressure of the gas doubles.
We can express this law in the form of an equation:

$$\frac{P_1}{T_1} = \frac{P_2}{T_2}$$

Example

A tin can at 27°C is heated to 327°C. If the initial pressure inside the can was 1 atmosphere what is the final pressure?

$$P_1 = 1 \text{ atm} \qquad P_2 = ?$$
$$T_1 = 27°C\,(300\,K) \qquad T_2 = 327°C\,(600\,K)$$

Using $\dfrac{P_1}{T_1} = \dfrac{P_2}{T_2}$

$$\therefore \frac{1\text{ atm}}{300\text{ K}} = \frac{P_2}{600\text{ K}}$$

$$\therefore P_2 = \frac{600}{300}\text{ atm} = \underline{\underline{2\text{ atm}}}$$

Charles' Law

To investigate the relationship between the volume of a gas and its temperature whilst the pressure remains constant

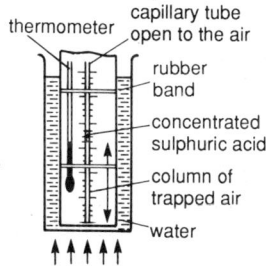

1. A fixed mass of gas, maintained at atmospheric pressure, is trapped inside a capillary tube by a bead of sulphuric acid.
2. The apparatus is put into a beaker of water whose temperature can be varied. The temperature and corresponding volume of gas are noted and recorded in a table, and a graph of volume against temperature is plotted.

58 Kinetic theory and heat

Typical results

Volume/cm^3	Temperature/°C	Temperature/K	$\dfrac{V/cm^3}{T/K}$
10.0	27	300	0.033
10.6	47	320	0.033
11.0	57	330	0.033
11.7	77	350	0.033
12.3	97	370	0.033

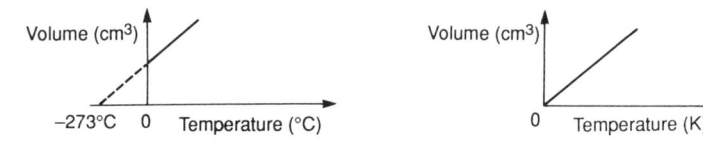

From the table and graphs we can see that
(a) V/T = a constant and
(b) there is a direct proportionality between volume and temperature providing the temperature is expressed in kelvin.

This relationship between the volume and temperature of a gas, is described by **Charles' Law** which states;

> The volume of a fixed mass of gas is directly proportional to its temperature provided that the pressure remains constant.

Charles' Law and Kinetic Theory

If the temperature of a gas (in kelvin) is doubled, the rate at which the gas molecules collide with the side of the container will double. If the pressure is to be kept constant the volume must also double, i.e. the volume is direcetly proportional to the temperature.

We can express this law in the form of an equation:

$$\frac{V_1}{T_1} = \frac{V_2}{T_2}$$

Temperature must be in kelvin.

Example

The temperature inside a hot air balloon of volume 200 m³ was 27°C. What would be the volume of the balloon if the temperature inside were raised to 127°C, assuming its pressure remains constant?

$$V_1 = 200 \text{ m}^3 \qquad V_2 = ?$$
$$T_1 = 27°C \text{ (300 K)} \qquad T_2 = 127°C \text{ (400 K)}$$

Using $\dfrac{V_1}{T_1} = \dfrac{V_2}{T_2}$

$$\dfrac{200 \text{ m}^3}{300 \text{ K}} = \dfrac{V_2}{400 \text{ K}}$$

$$\therefore V_2 = \dfrac{200 \times 400}{300} \text{ m}^3 = \underline{\underline{267 \text{ m}^3}}$$

Gas Law

In everyday life, it is likely that all three quantities (p, V and T) will alter. To deal with this situation, we use the equation on the right.

$$\boxed{\dfrac{p_1 V_1}{T_1} = \dfrac{p_2 V_2}{T_2}}$$

Example

A hot air balloon has a volume of 1000 m³, a temperature of 27°C and is at a pressure of 1 atm. If the temperature becomes 127°C and the pressure increases to 1.2 atm, what is the volume of the balloon now?

$$p_1 = 1 \text{ atm} \qquad p_2 = 1.2 \text{ atm}$$
$$V_1 = 1000 \text{ m}^3 \qquad V_2 = ?$$
$$T_1 = 27°C \text{ (300 K)} \qquad T_1 = 127°C \text{ (400 K)}$$

Using $\dfrac{p_1 V_1}{T_1} = \dfrac{p_2 V_2}{T_2}$

$$\therefore \dfrac{1 \text{ atm} \times 1000 \text{ m}^3}{300 \text{ K}} = \dfrac{1.2 \text{ atm} \times V_2}{400 \text{ K}}$$

$$\therefore V_2 = \dfrac{400 \times 1 \times 1000}{300 \times 1.2} \text{ m}^3 = \underline{\underline{1111 \text{ m}^3}}$$

KINETIC THEORY AND HEAT
4.8 Conduction and convection

4

There are three ways in which heat can travel – conduction, convection and radiation.

Conduction

If one end of a metal rod is held in a fire, heat is gradually conducted along it until the whole of the rod is warm.

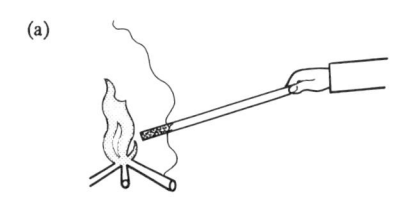

(a) Atoms and electrons which are being held in the fire gain energy and vibrate more vigorously.

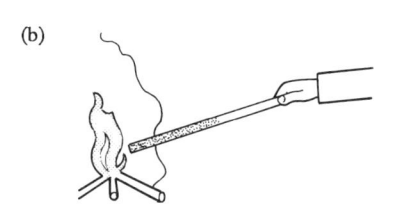

(b) This extra movement disturbs neighbouring cooler atoms and electrons further up the rod, causing them to vibrate more, i.e. they too become warm.

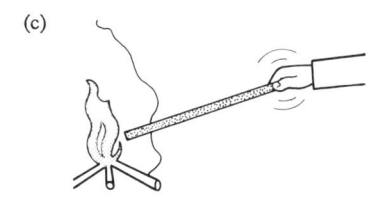

(c) Gradually this disturbance travels to the far end of the rod, i.e. heat has been conducted along the rod.

Comparing the conductivities of different metals

1 A marble is stuck with wax an equal distance from the end of four bars made from different metals.
2 The other ends of the bars are heated.
3 The marble falls first from the bar which is the best conductor.

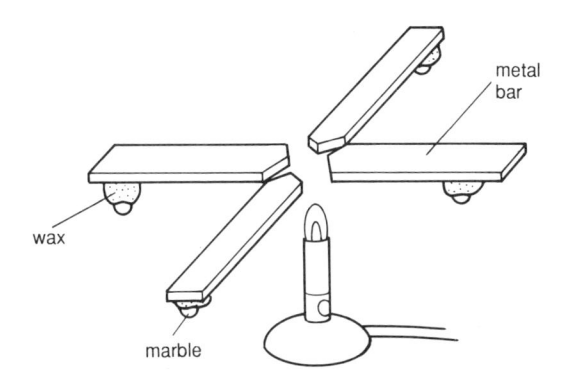

If a piece of paper is wrapped around this metal/wooden rod and heated gently, the paper in contact with the wood soon singes and becomes brown. The paper in contact with the metal remains undamaged. This happens because the metal rod rapidly conducts the heat from the paper, preventing it from burning. The wood does not conduct the heat away as rapidly and so the paper burns.

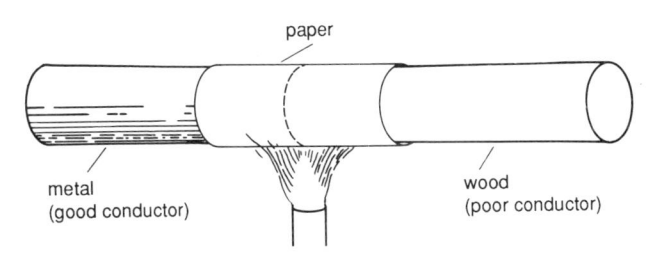

62 *Kinetic theory and heat*

Insulators

Keeping your feet warm in winter can be a problem, particularly if there is snow on the ground. One solution is to wear special shoes like moon-boots. The soles of these boots are made from an **insulator**. This is a material which does not allow heat to pass through it easily. Examples of insulators include wood, plastics, man-made fibres, wool and so on.

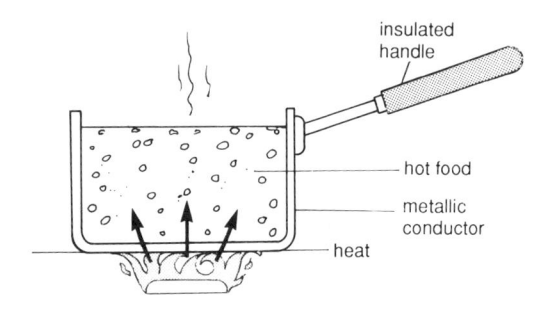

Heat transfers easily through the metal pan to warm the food. The insulated handle however remains cool.

Q Why, when we hold a knife does the plastic handle feel warm yet the metal blade feel cold?

Conduction in liquids

Water, like most liquids, is a poor conductor of heat. It is so poor that with a little care it is possible to have frozen water and boiling water in the same container separated by just a few centimetres.

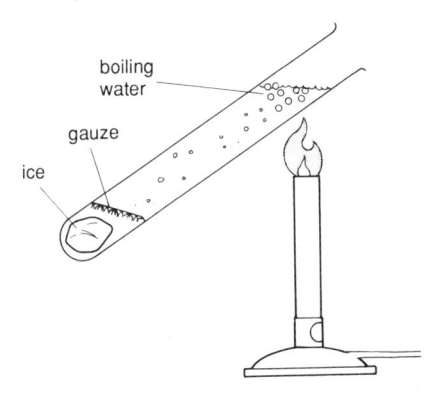

Conduction in gases

Gases are even poorer conductors of heat than liquids. They are in fact excellent insulators and often used to reduce the movement of heat.

In winter birds often fluff up their feathers. This traps layers of air which reduce the rate at which heat is lost from their bodies. Our winter clothing often uses the same principle, e.g. string vest, woolly jumpers, padded clothing filled with man-made fibres.

Glass fibre is an excellent material for insulating lofts. It contains large quantities of trapped air which reduce heat loss.

Double glazing reduces the rate at which heat escapes through windows. It is the insulating properties of the air trapped between the two panes of glass which achieve this.

Convection

Convection can occur only in liquids and gases.

Convection in liquids

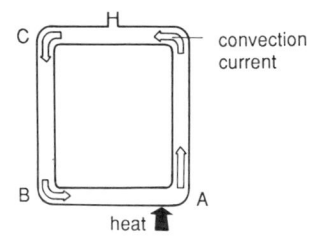

(a) As the liquid is heated at A it becomes less dense and rises.

(b) Cooler liquid moves in from B to take the place of the rising, less dense liquid.

(c) Away from the heat source the liquid begins to cool at C, becomes more dense and so falls.

Domestic hot water system

Some of the older domestic hot water systems depend upon convection currents to move the hot water around the house.
(a) The water which has been heated in the boiler rises and travels through pipe A into the top of the hot water cylinder.
(b) Cooler water from the bottom of the hot water cylinder falls through pipe B into the boiler where it is reheated.
(c) If water is drawn off through pipe C to the taps it is replaced by cold water from the cold water storage tank, through pipe D.

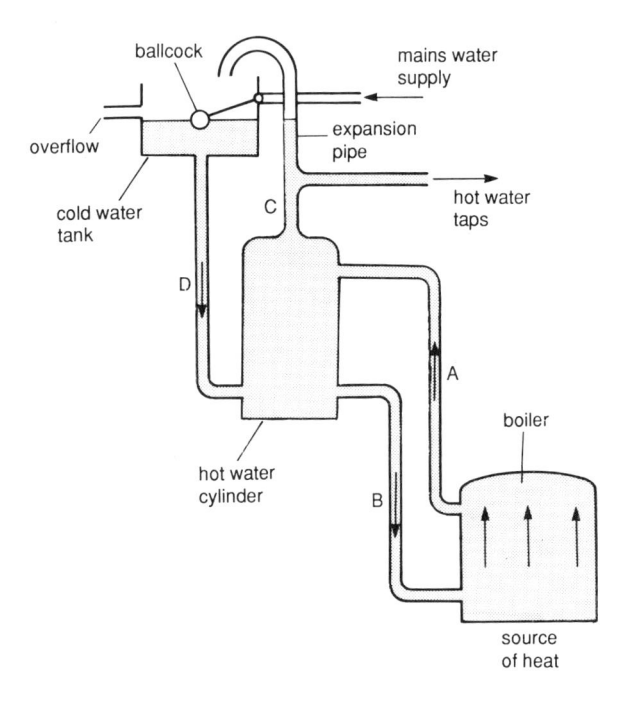

Q Why is hot water taken from and fed into the top of the cylinder or boiler whilst cold water is taken from and fed into the bottom of the cylinder and boiler?
Why do modern systems not have to depend upon convection currents to move hot water around the house?

Kinetic theory and heat 65

Convection in gases

Convection currents are often set up by the sun along the coast. During the day the land warms up more quickly than the sea. The air above the land therefore becomes warm and rises. Cooler air from the sea then moves in to take the place of the rising air, i.e. an onshore breeze is set up.

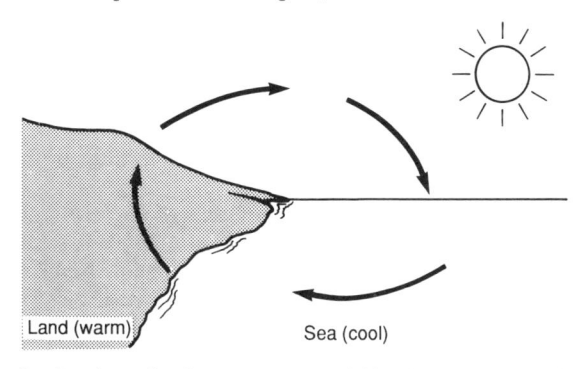

At night the land cools down more rapidly than the sea. The air immediately above the sea is now warmer and so rises. The cooler air from the land then moves in to take its place, i.e. an offshore breeze is set up.

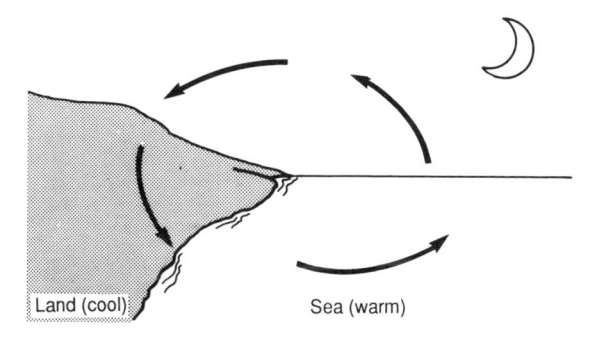

Q Explain why the heater is placed at the bottom of an oven and yet the freezing compartment of a refrigerator is at the top.

KINETIC THEORY AND HEAT
4.9 Radiation

The energy we receive from the Sun travels as electromagnetic radiation. It does not involve the movement of molecules and is therefore the only means by which heat can travel through a vacuum.

Absorbing radiation

When radiation strikes an object some of it will be absorbed while the rest of it will be reflected. How much energy is absorbed is determined by the nature of the object's surface.

Objects which have *dark, rough* surfaces absorb most of the radiation and reflect very little.

Objects which have *light, smooth* surfaces absorb very little radiation, and reflect most of it.

For example, the dark surfaces of the canopy below have absorbed the sun's radiation, become warm and so have lost their icicles. The lighter surfaces have reflected most of the radiation, remained cool and so still have their icicles. This can be a useful property: the silvery surface of a fireman's suit reflects the heat, keeping him cool, and in hot countries houses are often painted white to keep them cool.

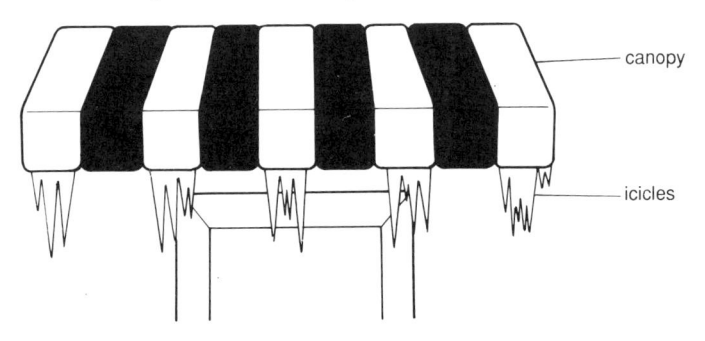

Emitters of radiation

All warm objects give off (lose) energy in the form of radiation. They are **emitters.**

Objects which have *dark, rough* surfaces are good emitters of heat. Objects which have *light, smooth* surfaces are poor emitters of heat. For example, the outside of a silver teapot is shiny and smooth: very little heat is emitted and so the tea stays warm. In the same way in order to stop a motorbike engine from overheating, its casing is surrounded with cooling fins. Painting these black helps them lose energy more quickly.

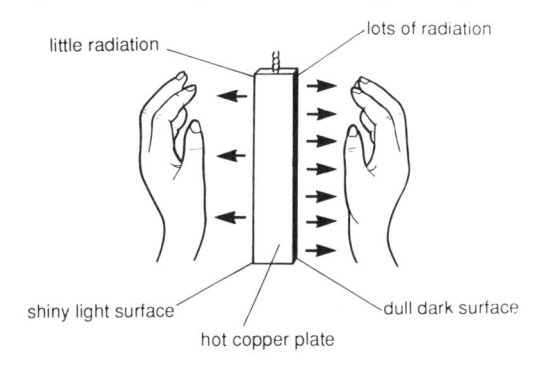

KINETIC THEORY AND HEAT
4.10 Uses of heat transfer

The vacuum flask

This is designed to prevent heat flowing into or out of it.

(a) Heat moving by conduction or convection cannot travel through the vacuum.
(b) Any radiation which crosses the vacuum is reflected back by a silvered surface.
(c) The silvered surfaces also reduce the amount of heat being radiated.
(d) The stopper is made of an insulator such as cork or plastic.
(e) The outer case is usually made of plastic which is a poor conductor of heat.

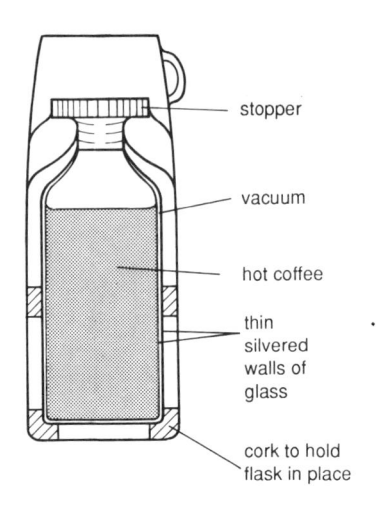

The greenhouse effect

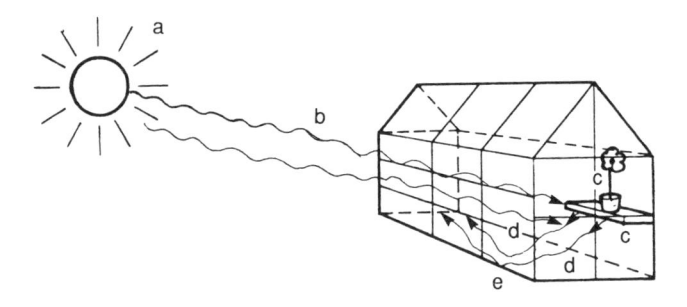

(a) Short wavelength radiation (infra-red) is emitted by the sun.
(b) This short-wave radiation passes through the greenhouse glass.
(c) Objects inside the greenhouse absorb the sun's radiation and become warm.
(d) Longer wavelength radiation is emitted by these objects.
(e) The longer wavelength radiation is unable to pass through the sheets of glass and so the heat is trapped inside the greenhouse.

Scientists are at present concerned that the burning of fossil fuels is increasing the level of carbon dioxide in the atmosphere. This acts like the glass of the greenhouse and traps the long wavelength radiation, so there is a fear that the Earth is gradually becoming warmer.

Q What effect might this have
   (a) on global weather patterns?
   (b) on the Arctic and Antarctic?

Insulating the home

The diagram below shows how heat is lost from a house if no attempt is made to insulate it. The percentages given are approximate.

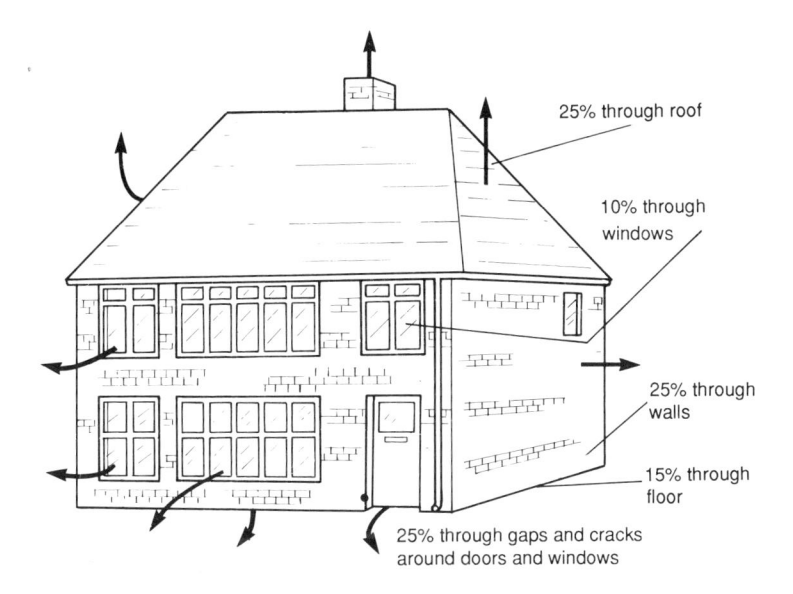

- 25% through roof
- 10% through windows
- 25% through walls
- 15% through floor
- 25% through gaps and cracks around doors and windows

Much of this heat loss can be reduced by:
(a) injecting foam between cavity walls (the foam is an excellent insulator and prevents convection currents between the walls);
(b) insulating the loft with fibreglass;
(c) fitting underlay and carpets to reduce heat loss through the floor;
(d) double glazing all windows;
(e) eliminating cracks around doors and windows to reduce heat loss by convection.

KINETIC THEORY AND HEAT
4.11 Questions

4

1. When clothes have been washed they are often hung out to dry.
   (i) What is happening to the water in clothes when they are hung out to dry?
   (ii) Select from the words below the ideal conditions for drying clothes. Explain why each of the conditions you chose helps the clothes to dry.

humid	still	windy	hot
dry	raining	frosty	cloudy

2. Explain in detail how a radiator is able to warm the whole of the room it is in.
   What would be the effect of
   (i) painting the radiator black?
   (ii) placing silver foil between the radiator and the wall?
   (iii) making the radiator and water pipes out of white plastic?
   (iv) fixing the radiator high on the wall (just under the ceiling)?
   Some radiators have thermostatic valves attached to them. What do they do and why are they useful?

3. **A** When a gas cools it loses energy.
   B When a gas condenses it loses energy.
   C When a liquid cools it loses energy.
   D Energy always flows from high temperatures to lower temperatures.
   Using the above statements answer the questions below.
   (i) Which way does heat energy flow if
      (a) hot water is spilt on someone's hand?
      (b) fresh meat is put into a freezer?
      (c) a cake is moved from the bottom of the oven to the top?
   (ii) Scalding with steam causes more damage to skin than boiling water. Explain why this is so. To minimise the injury, it is important to remove energy as quickly as possible from the burned area. Suggest how this might be done.

4. The specific heat capacity of water is 4200 J/(KgK). How much energy is needed to raise the temperature of 0.4 kg of water from 10°C to 50°C?

5

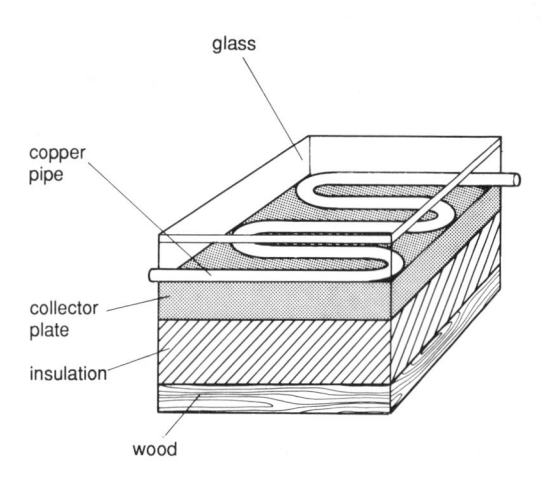

This diagram shows the basic structure of a solar panel. It uses the heat from the Sun to warm water which flows through the pipes.
(i) Why is the pipe fixed to a dark-coloured collector plate?
(ii) Why is the pipe made of copper?
(iii) Why is the pipe made to zigzag up and down?
(iv) Why is the collector plate fixed to an insulator?
Suggest a suitable material which could be used for the insulation.
(v) Why is the panel front covered with glass?
(vi) Suggest one advantage of double glazing the front of the panel.

WAVES
5.1 Wave properties

In everyday life we come into contact with many different kinds of waves. We use light waves to see. We use radio and sound waves to communicate. We use microwaves to cook. We use water waves when we surf.

A wave is in fact a means by which energy can be transferred from place to place. For example, over 99% of the energy which all animals and plants need to survive comes from the Sun in the form of waves.

By studying the basic common properties of waves, we can learn to make maximum use of their benefits whilst minimising their harmful properties.

There are two main groups of waves:
(a) transverse waves and
(b) longitudinal waves.

A **transverse wave** is one in which the vibrations (displacements) are at right angles to the direction in which the wave is moving. Examples of such waves include water waves, light waves and pulses in a rope or string (shown below).

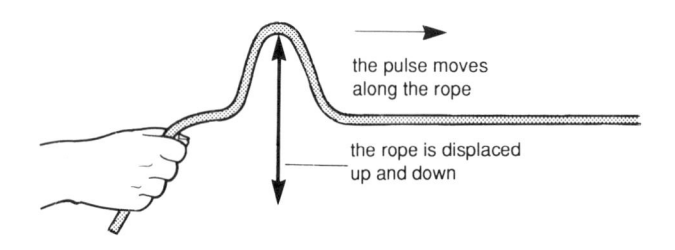

If pulses are created at regular intervals the waves will look like this:

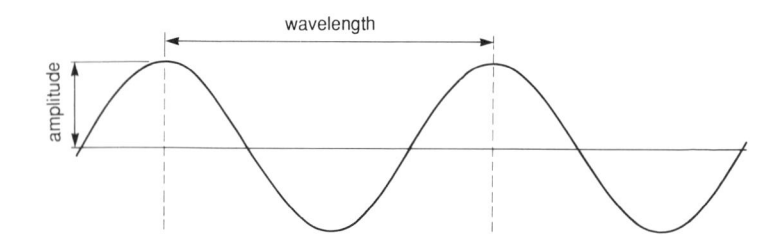

The maximum displacement is called the **amplitude** of the wave. The distance between two successive peaks or crests is called the **wavelength**.

All waves begin as vibrations. The object producing the wave vibrates at a rate which is called the **frequency** of the wave. This is measured in **hertz**. For example an object which completes one vibration every second (and therefore produces one complete wave each second) has a frequency of one hertz (1 Hz).

A **longitudinal** wave is one in which the vibrations are in the same direction as the wave is moving.

If a single push pulse is sent through a slinky it will look like this:

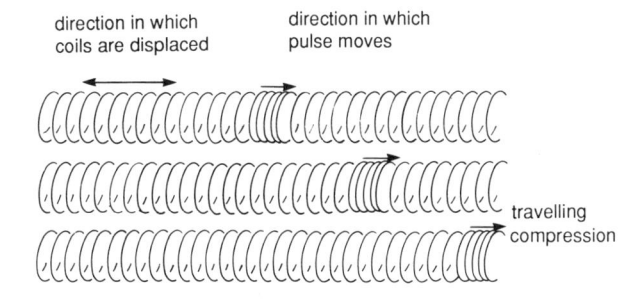

direction in which coils are displaced

direction in which pulse moves

travelling compression

If pulses are sent through a slinky at regular intervals it will look like this:

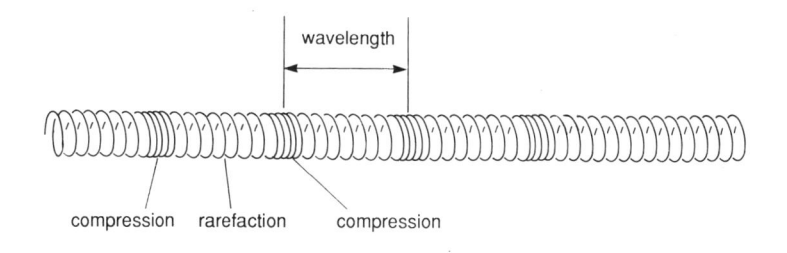

wavelength

compression   rarefaction   compression

Sound waves are longitudinal waves (see page 78). One of the most convenient ways to study waves is to use a ripple tank.

74 *Waves*

The ripple tank

When the small motor is turned on the wooden bar vibrates, causing a regular series of ripples to be created in the water. Shadows of these ripples can be cast on the floor or ceiling and the behaviour of the waves easily observed.

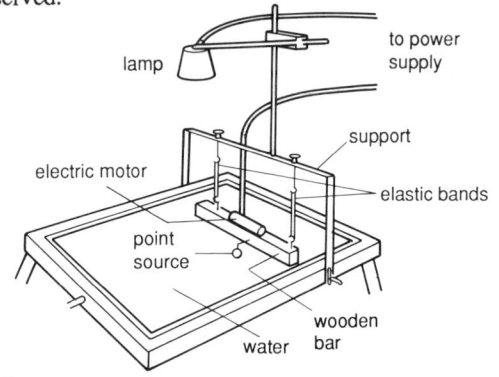

Sources of waves

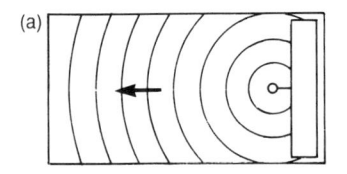

(a) A point source produces circular wavefronts.

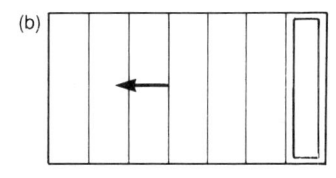

(b) A flat or plane source produces plane waves.

Frequency and wavelength

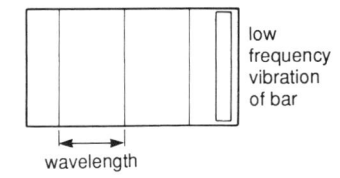

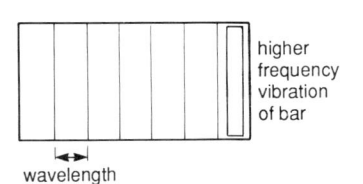

low frequency vibration of bar — wavelength

higher frequency vibration of bar — wavelength

The higher the frequency of the source, the shorter the wavelength of the waves produced.

Reflection

Plane and curved barriers show very clearly how waves can be reflected in different ways.

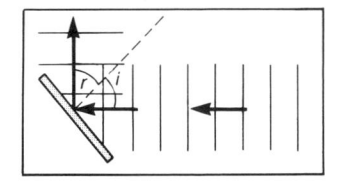

Reflection from a plane or flat barrier. angle i = angle r.

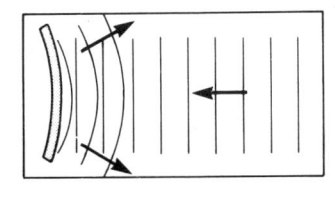

Reflection from a convex or diverging barrier.

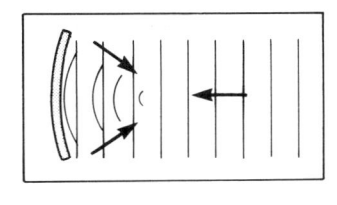

Reflection from a concave or converging barrier.

Refraction

As the waves move into shallower water (dark area in the diagram) they are slowed down. This causes the waves to change direction or **refract**.

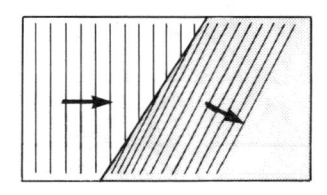

Refraction of plane waves

Diffraction

As the waves move through a narrow gap they spread out. This spreading out is called **diffraction.**

If the width of the gap is similar to the wavelength of the waves, the diffraction is greatest.

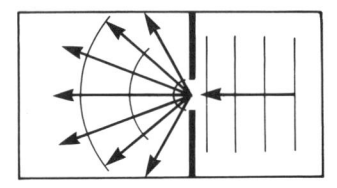

If the width of the gap is larger than the wavelength of the waves, the diffraction is less.

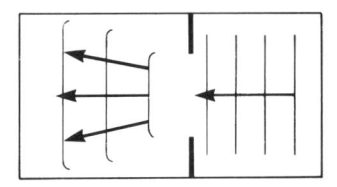

Interference

If two wave sources are used they will each produce their own wave pattern. The two sets of waves will overlap and **interfere** with each other, as shown below.

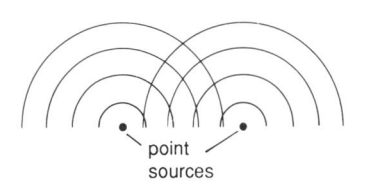

Overlapping waves

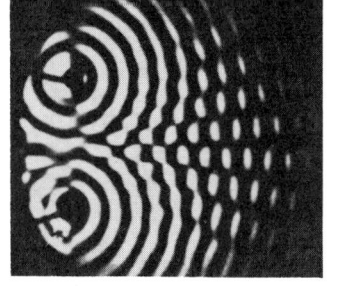

Resulting interference pattern.

In those places where the peaks of two waves or the troughs of two waves overlap we will get **constructive interference**.

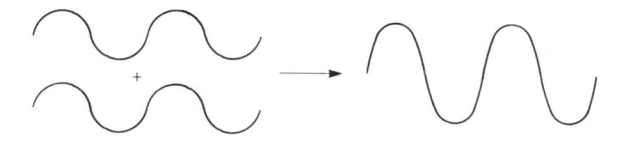

But in those places where the peaks of one wave overlap with the troughs of a second wave we will get **destructive interference**.

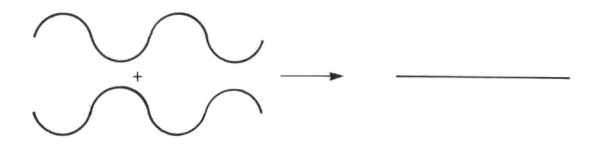

The wave equation

From the first ripple tank diagrams we can see that if the frequency of vibration is high the waves are close together, i.e. they have a short wavelength. If the frequency of vibration is low the waves are more spread out, i.e. they have a longer wavelength. This happens because the wavelength and frequency of any wave are related to each other by the following equation.

$$v = f\lambda$$

where v is the wave velocity
f is the wave frequency
λ is the wavelength

Example

A signal generator emits a sound wave of wavelength 2 m. If the speed of sound is 340 m/s what is the frequency of this wave?

Using $v = f\lambda$,

$$340 \, \text{m/s} = f \times 2 \, \text{m}$$

$$\therefore f = \frac{340}{2} \text{Hz}$$

$$= 170 \, \text{Hz}$$

WAVES
5.2 Sound waves

All sounds begin with an object vibrating, e.g. the strings of a guitar, the skin of a drum, the reed of a clarinet, etc. If the object is large, such as a string of a double bass, it will vibrate slowly and produce a low pitched note. If, however, the object is small, such as one of the strings on a violin, it will vibrate rapidly, and produce a high pitched note.

Large musical instruments produce low pitched notes.

Smaller musical instruments produce higher pitched notes.

How sound waves move

As an object vibrates back and forth it pushes the air molecules close to it, creating a series of moving compressions and rarefactions which we call a sound wave (see slinky, page 73).

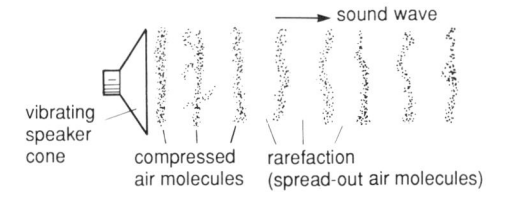

Transmission of sound waves

Sound waves can travel through solids, liquids or gases; i.e. they can travel through any medium providing there are atoms or molecules present. If there are no atoms or molecules present, i.e. the medium is a vacuum, the sound waves are unable to travel through it.

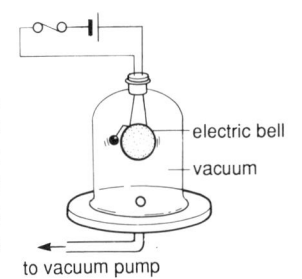

When the air is pumped out no sound can be heard.

Speed of sound

Measuring the speed of sound

1. Two pieces of wood are banged together to produce a sharp, crisp sound. At the same instant a stopwatch is started.
2. When the echo is heard the stopwatch is stopped and the time recorded.
3. The experiment is repeated and an average value for the timings of the echo calculated.
4. The distance the sound has travelled – from the source to the reflecting surface and back – is accurately measured.
5. A value for the speed of sound can then be calculated using the equation

$$\text{speed} = \frac{\text{distance travelled}}{\text{time}}$$

At sea level the speed of sound is approximately 340 m/s.

Supersonic

Many of today's military aircraft are supersonic, i.e. they can travel faster than sound. As an aircraft accelerates through this speed, it catches up with and passes through the sound waves it is creating. As it does so we say that it is going through the sound barrier.

Using echoes

Ships often use echoes – SONAR (SOund Navigation And Ranging) – to discover how deep the ocean is or to detect shoals of fish. They have even been used to try to prove the existence of the Loch Ness Monster.

The ship sends a sound wave down to the sea-bed and then notes how quickly the echo returns. If the echo returns quickly this shows that there is a large object – or animal?!! – beneath the ship.

Similarly bats emit high-pitched sounds and use their echoes in order to avoid flying into objects and to detect their prey.

80 *Waves*

Example

A bat hears an echo from a flying insect after 0.5 s. If the speed of sound is 340 m/s how far is the bat from its prey?

$$\text{speed} = \frac{\text{distance}}{\text{time}}$$

$$\text{distance} = \text{speed} \times \text{time}$$

$$= 340 \text{ m/s} \times 0.5 \text{ s}$$

$$= 170 \text{m}$$

The bat is therefore 85 m from its prey.

Musical qualities of sound: pitch, loudness and quality

Although we can't see sound waves we can, by using a Cathode Ray Oscilloscope (CRO), observe what happens to a sound when we change its pitch, loudness or quality.

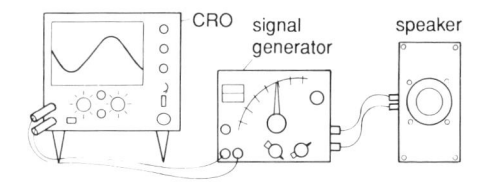

Pitch In music rather than talking about the frequency of a note we talk about its pitch. The two are very similar in that a high pitched note has a high frequency of vibration.

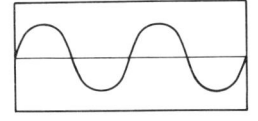

Low pitched sound

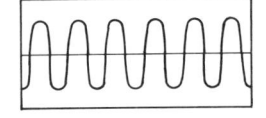

High pitched sound

Loudness or amplitude The loudness of a note depends upon the number of air molecules hitting our eardrums at any one time. The more molecules that do this the louder the note. A loud note is seen on the CRO as a tall wave, i.e. it has a large amplitude.

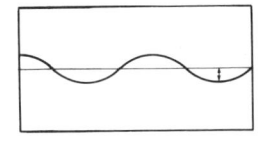

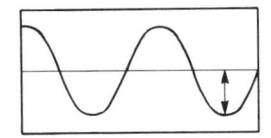

Quiet sound   Loud sound

We measure the loudness of sound in **decibels** (dB). A sound which is so quiet that we can only just hear it, has a loudness of 0 dB. Normal conversation has a loudness of 20 dB. Someone shouting has a loudness of 100 dB. A rock concert has a loudness of 120 dB. A noise so loud that it may cause permanent damage to one's hearing has a loudness of 140 dB.

Q What are ear protectors? Who might wear them?

Timbre or quality If two musical instruments such as a piano and a trumpet play the same note one after another, it is very easy for us to recognise which instrument played which note. This is because although the two notes have the same pitch and loudness, they have different *timbre* or *quality*. Notes of different timbre have waves of different shapes. This difference in shape is due to the presence of *overtones* and *harmonics*.

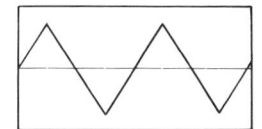

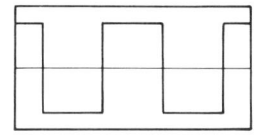

Sounds with the same frequency but having different timbre or quality.

Ultrasonics

Sound waves which have a frequency greater than 20 000 Hz cannot be detected by the human ear. These waves can therefore be used to convey signals without disturbing anyone who may be listening, e.g. a dog whistle.

Ultrasonic waves are also used in medicine to observe things not visible to the naked eye, e.g. the state of growth of babies whilst still in the womb, the workings of the heart, or the position of tumours.

Q Why might a doctor use ultrasonic waves rather than X-rays to investigate these things?

WAVES
5.3 Light: reflection

5

Rays of light

Light is a form of energy. It is emitted from objects such as fires, light bulbs, stars, etc. but most of our light comes from the Sun. Light travels in straight lines, so we can draw it as rays.

We see **luminous** objects like the Sun because of the light they emit. **Non-luminous** objects we see because of the light they reflect. Without light we would be unable to see.

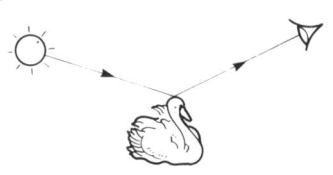

Reflection

When a ray of light hits a plane mirror the direction in which it is reflected can always be predicted, as the **angle of incidence** (i) = the **angle of reflection** (r).

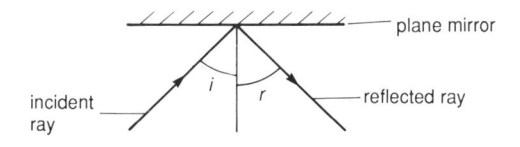

The diagram below shows how a plane mirror creates an **image** of an object. The brain believes that the rays of light have come from I. It therefore sees an image of the object O at I. The rays of light do not actually pass through the image. It is therefore known as a **virtual** image.

Images through which rays of light pass are known as **real** images.

The image created by a plane mirror is always
(a) upright;
(b) the same size as the object;
(c) the same distance behind the mirror as the object is in front;
(d) laterally inverted;
(e) virtual

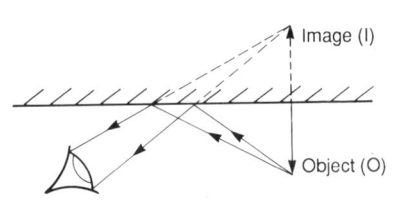

Plane mirrors are also used to change the direction in which a ray of light is moving, e.g. in a simple periscope.

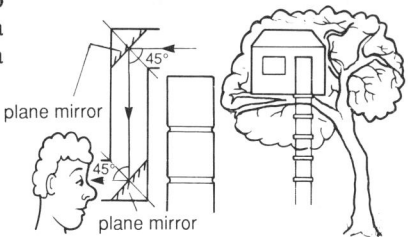

Curved mirrors

Sometimes we can obtain a more useful image if the surface of a mirror is curved. The rays of light are still reflected so that the angle of incidence equals the angle of reflection, but the curved surface causes the rays to converge or diverge.

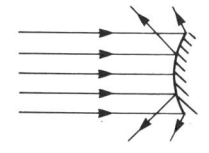

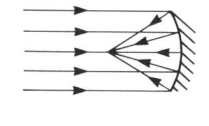

Converging concave mirror   Diverging convex mirror

In the bathroom if we shave or put on make up it is useful to use a concave mirror which produces a magnified upright image. Keeping an eye on the traffic behind us is much easier if our rear view mirror has a convex curve. This enables us to have a much wider field of vision.

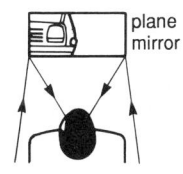

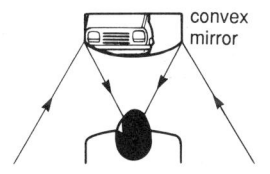

Q Where and why might convex mirrors be used in shops?

Parabolic mirrors

These have a special shape and are often used in torches, car headlamps, search-lights, etc. in order to reflect the rays into a parallel beam.

WAVES
5.4 Light: refraction

Spearing this fish is not quite as easy as it first seems. Rays of light from the fish have changed direction as they crossed the water/air boundary. The fisherman therefore sees the fish at B rather than A. An experienced hunter will allow for this optical deception – an inexperienced one may not and so will miss the fish.

This change in direction of a ray is called **refraction** and happens because light travels more quickly in air than in water. Similarly, if a stick is partly immersed in water it appears bent so that an observer will see the end of the stick at B rather than A. Refraction also causes streams, ponds, etc., to look shallower than they really are.

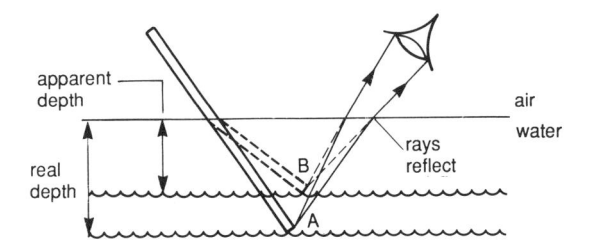

When a ray of light passes through a window it is refracted twice – once as it enters the glass and again as it leaves. Because windows are quite thin the effect is hardly noticeable. If, however, we observe an object through a thick glass block the effect is very noticeable.

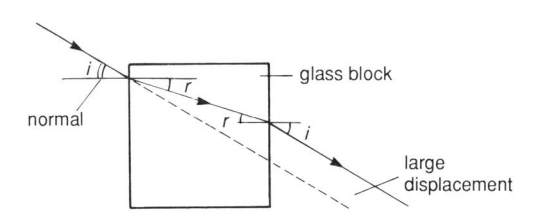

i = angle of incidence
r = angle of refraction

Dispersion of white light by refraction

If a ray of white light enters a prism it emerges as a band of colours called a **spectrum**. This effect is called **dispersion**.

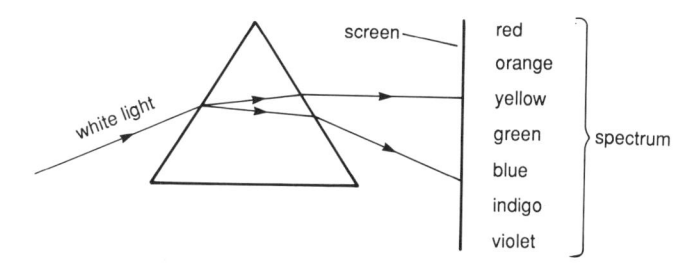

At each of the two surfaces of the prism the coloured lights are refracted by different amounts – those with high frequencies (violet) are bent the most whilst those with low frequencies (red) are bent the least.

A second inverted prism can be used to recombine the colours of the spectrum to form white light.

Rainbows are also created by the dispersion of white light by refraction. The refraction, however, is not by a glass prism but by water droplets in the atmosphere.

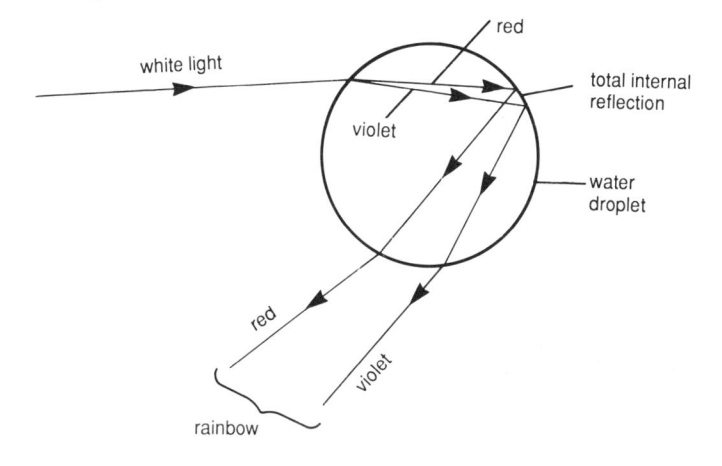

WAVES
5.5 Total internal reflection

Sometimes when a ray of light is about to travel out of a more optically dense medium, the ray is reflected by the boundary as if it were a mirror instead of passing through. This phenomenon is called **total internal reflection.**

Total internal reflection only occurs when
(a) a ray is travelling from a more optically dense medium into a less optically dense medium, e.g. glass to air;
(b) it strikes the boundary between the two media at an angle greater than the **critical angle** (c).

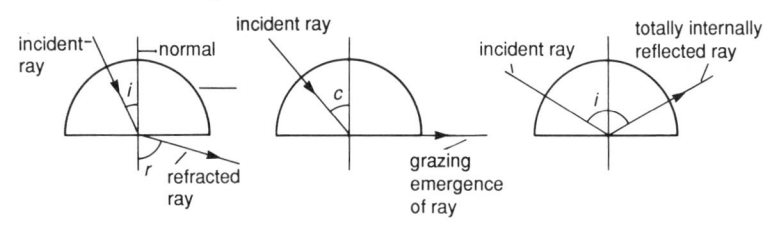

(i) Angle of incidence less than the critical angle

(ii) Angle of incidence equal to the critical angle

(iii) Angle of incidence greater than the critical angle

Different materials have different critical angles,

e.g. glass   42.0°
      perspex   42.2°
      alcohol   47.3°

Prismatic periscope

Prismatic periscopes use prisms to reflect the light rather than mirrors, as they produce a brighter final image.

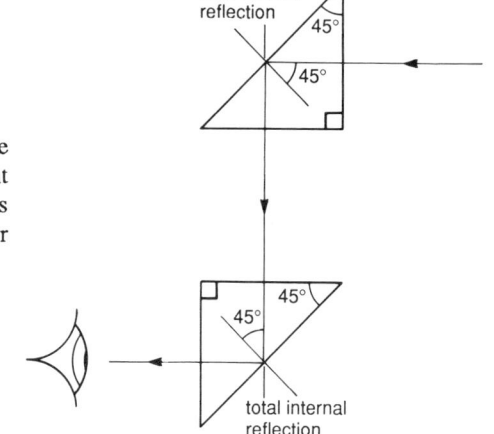

Prismatic binoculars

Prismatic binoculars are really squashed up telescopes. Their length is kept to a minimum by reflecting the rays back and forth using prisms.

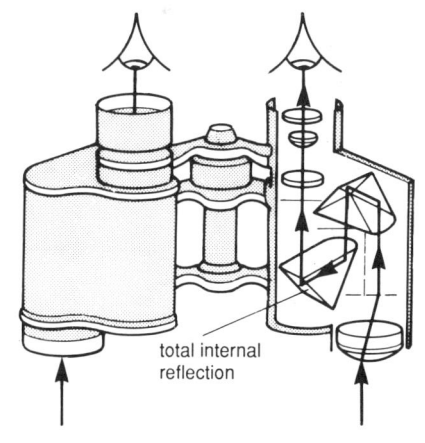

total internal reflection

Optical fibres

Optical fibres are designed to conduct or pipe rays of light along curved paths. Light entering a fibre is unable to escape as it undergoes multiple total internal reflections until it emerges at the far end as shown below.

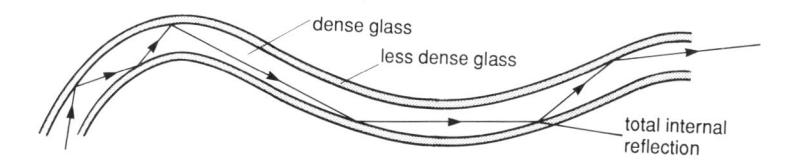

dense glass
less dense glass
total internal reflection

If several thousand of these fibres are grouped together they form a flexible light pipe which can be used by doctors to see inside a patient's body.

Optical fibres are also used in telecommunications. They are much cheaper than copper wires and can carry far more messages.

WAVES
5.6 Lenses

A lens is a specially shaped piece of glass or plastic which refracts light in a predictable and useful way. Contact lenses and the lenses in spectacles help people with eye defects to see clearly. There are two main types of lens.

Convex or converging lens
This bends the rays of light in such a way as to cause them to converge.

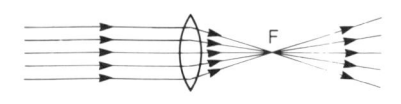

Concave or diverging lens
This bends the rays of light in such a way as to cause them to diverge.

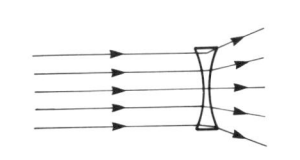

Parts of a lens

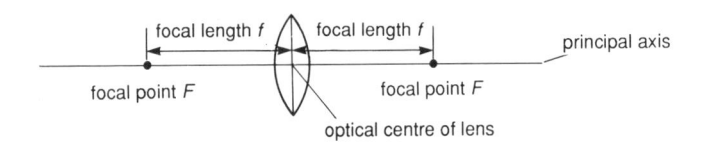

Ray diagrams

For a convex lens there are three particular rays whose behaviour can be predicted.

(a) A ray which travels parallel to the principal axis will, on being refracted by the lens, pass through the far focal point.
(b) A ray which passes through one of the focal points before entering the lens will be refracted parallel to the principal axis.
(c) A ray which passes through the optical centre of the lens will be undeviated.

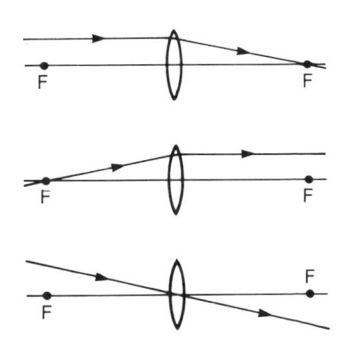

Focal points

If we want to use a lens in an optical instrument such as a telescope or microscope it is important that we choose one which bends the light by the correct amount. Lenses which have a short focal length bend light rays more than those that have a long focal length. Knowing the focal length of a lens would therefore help us to choose the correct lens for a particular optical instrument.

The focal point of a convex lens is the point on which rays travelling parallel to the principal axis converge after passing through the lens (see diagram on page 88).

To determine the focal length of a convex lens by the distant object method.

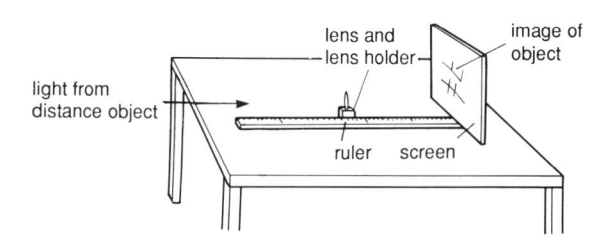

A screen placed behind the lens is moved back and forth until a sharp image of a distant object is obtained. The distance between the lens and the screen is now equal to the focal length of the lens.

This is a very quick method for finding the focal length of a convex lens but it is not very accurate.

To determine the focal length of a convex lens using a plane mirror.

A plane mirror is placed behind the lens. The cross-wires and screen are moved back and forth until a sharp image of the cross-wires is obtained on the screen. The distance between the screen and lens is now equal to the focal length.

This is a more accurate method than the distant object method.

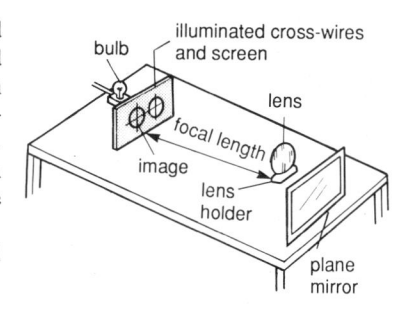

Convex lenses

Position of object	Position of image	Nature of image
Between focal point and lens	Only time it is the same side of lens as object	magnified upright virtual
At the focal point	At infinity	–
Between F and 2F	Between 2F and infinity	magnified inverted real
At 2F	At 2F – (the same distance on the other side of the lens)	same size inverted real
Between 2F and infinity	Between F and 2F	diminished inverted real
At infinity	At F	diminished inverted real

A convex lens can produce many different images. Some are real, some virtual, some magnified and some diminished. By using any two of the predictable rays we can draw ray diagrams to discover the nature and positions of images created by a convex lens as shown in the table above.

Ray diagram	Practical application
	Magnifying glass
	Spotlights
	Projector
	Terrestrial telescope (inverts the image so that it is upright)
	Camera
	Telescope (objective lens)

Concave lenses

The image created by a concave lens is always erect, diminished and virtual.

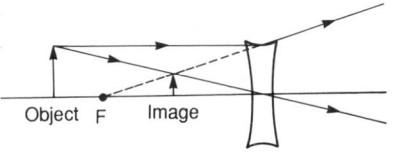

WAVES
5.7 Optical instruments

5

Pinhole camera

This consists of a lightproof box with a single pinhole in one side. Rays of light from an object enter the camera, creating an image on the far side of the box.

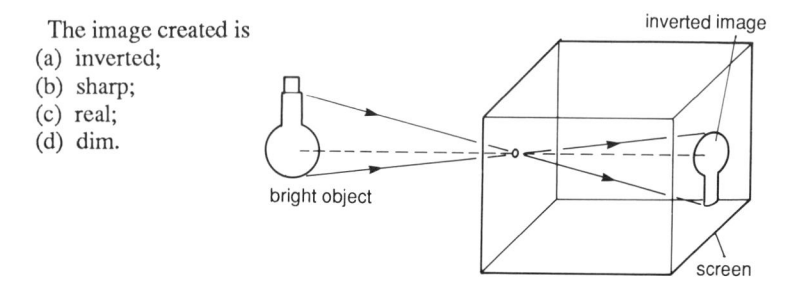

The image created is
(a) inverted;
(b) sharp;
(c) real;
(d) dim.

The biggest disadvantage with the pinhole camera is the dimness of the image. If the pinhole is made larger to allow more light to enter, the image becomes blurred.

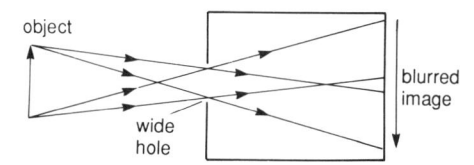

Camera

Twentieth century cameras have solved this problem by using lenses which make the image sharp even when the hole is quite large.

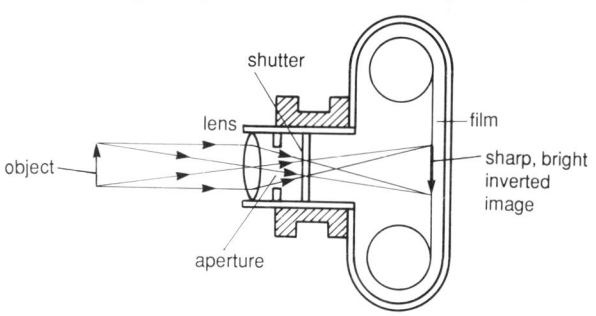

(a) Light from the object enters the camera through a hole behind the lens called the **aperture.**
(b) The light is focused by the lens to create a sharp image on the film. (The lens can normally be moved back and forth so that images of objects both near and far can be focused on the film.)
(c) When a photograph is taken the shutter opens and shuts rapidly, allowing light into the camera for a very short period of time – usually between $\frac{1}{60}$ s and $\frac{1}{500}$ s.
(d) If the film is to be correctly exposed the size of the aperture and the speed of the shutter have to be matched. Many cameras do this automatically although some photographers prefer to do it manually.

Magnifying glass

Providing the object is inside the focal length of the lens the image produced will be upright and magnified.

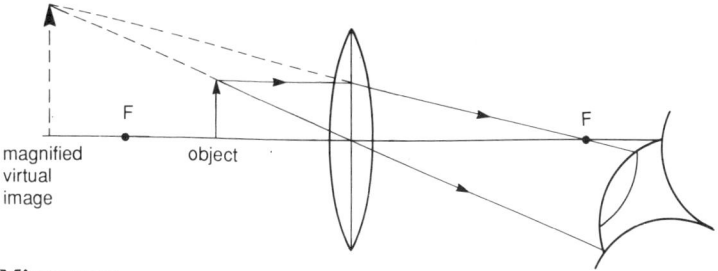

Microscope

Microscopes achieve a higher magnification by using a second lens to magnify the image created by the first.

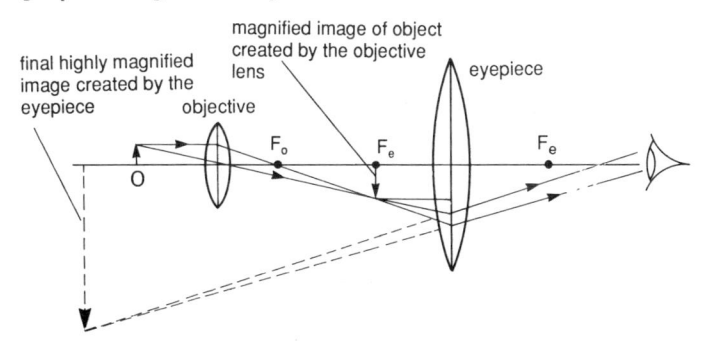

Refracting astronomical telescope

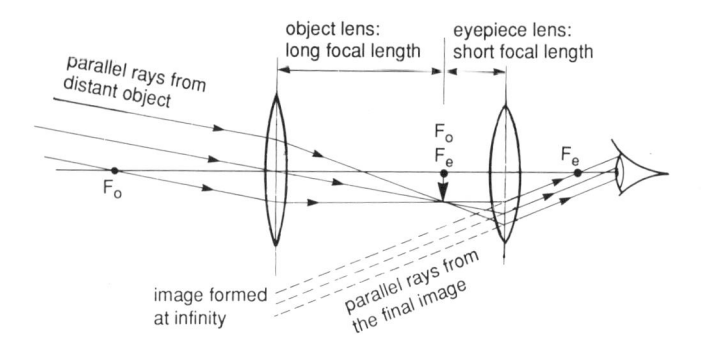

(a) Light from distant planets and stars arrives at the objective lens as a parallel beam.
(b) A real inverted image is created at the focal point of the objective.
(c) The eyepiece acts as a magnifying glass, forming a final magnified image.

Reflecting astronomical telescope

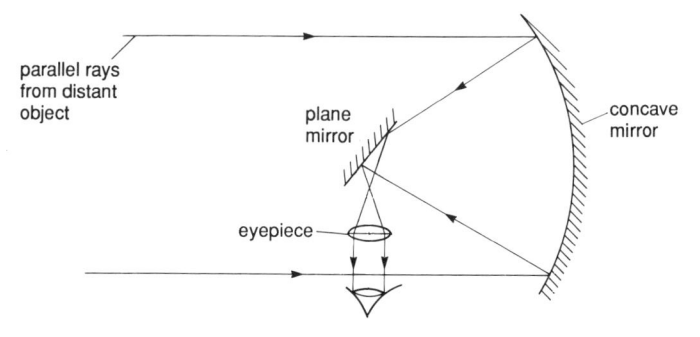

(a) A very large concave mirror collects and converges light from the distant object.
(b) The converging light is reflected by a plane mirror into a convex lens which forms the final magnified image.

Q The Mount Palomar Telescope in California has a concave mirror of diameter 5 m. Suggest one reason why such a large mirror is necessary.

Projector

Light from the lamp is concentrated onto the slide by the concave mirror and the condenser lenses. A magnified inverted image of the strongly illuminated slide is then projected on the screen by the convex projection lens. The distance between the projection lens and the slide can be altered in order to focus the image on the screen.

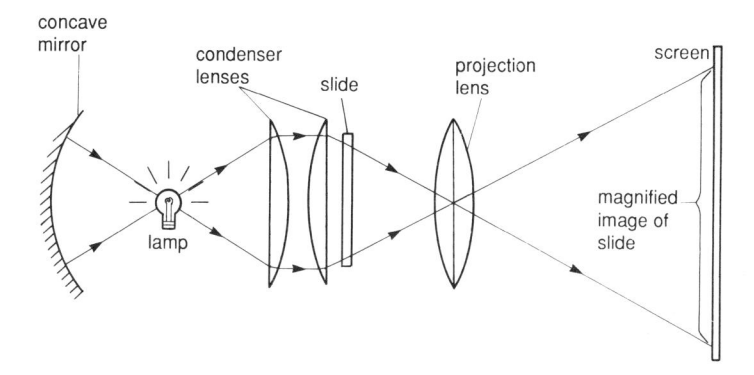

WAVES
5.8 The electromagnetic spectrum

5

Light travels in waves. It is part of a large family of waves called the **electromagnetic spectrum**. These waves consist of a magnetic field and an electric field vibrating at right angles to each other as shown below.

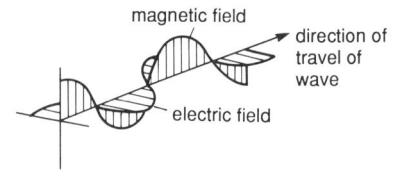

The table summarises the most important features of the different regions of the spectrum.

Type of wave	Gamma rays	X-rays	Ultra-violet waves
Wavelength	10^{-14} m	10^{-10} m	10^{-8} m
Frequency	10^{22} Hz	10^{18} Hz	10^{16} Hz
Source	Radioactive material	X-ray tube	Mercury lamp
Detection	Geiger tube	Photographic film	Photographic film. Causes some objects to fluoresce
Uses	Detecting flaws in metal castings. Medicine e.g. cancer treatment	Medical e.g. detection of broken bones	Lighting for sunbeds. Treatment of skin complaints

Although at first the different kinds of electromagnetic waves appear to have little in common, they do in fact have many important similarities.

(a) They all travel at the speed of light.
(b) They can all travel through a vacuum.
(c) They all exhibit basic wave properties, i.e. reflection, refraction, diffraction, interference, etc.
(d) They are all transverse waves.

Visible light	Infra-red waves	Microwaves	Radio waves
10^{-7} m	10^{-5} m	10^{-2} m	10^4 m
10^{15} Hz	10^{13} Hz	10^{10} Hz	10^4 Hz
Sun	Electric fire	Special electrical circuits	Transmitting aerials
Eye Photographic film	Touch Photographic film	Heating effect Radio receiver	Radio receiver
Photography To help us to see	Cooking Heating Photography	Microwave oven	Radio

WAVES
5.9 Questions

1

pupil

iris

ciliary muscles *lens*

pupil

retina

cornea

iris

liquid

optic nerve

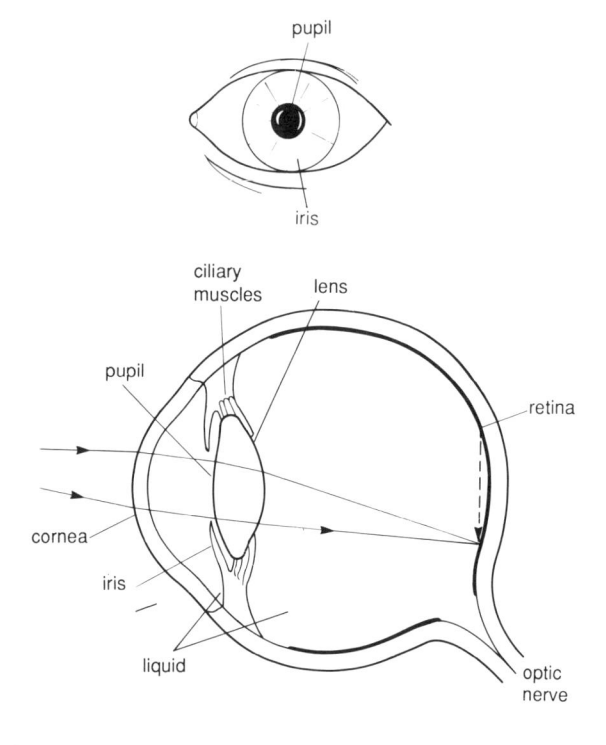

The diagram above shows the main parts of the eye. Rays of light which enter the eye are brought to focus on the **retina** by the eye lens. This image is then transmitted to the brain via the optic nerve.

If we look at a distant object the light rays coming from it need to be bent just a little in order to bring them together at the retina. To achieve this the shape of the lens is altered by the ciliary muscles so that it is long and thin.

If we look at an object which is close the light rays need to be bent quite a lot in order to bring them together at the retina. To achieve this the ciliary muscles make the lens short and fat.

(i) Draw a ray diagram of the eye observing
   (a) a distant object;
   (b) a near object.

The window (black hole) which allows light into the eye is called the **pupil**. If too much or too little light is entering the eye the pupil becomes smaller or larger.

(ii) Draw a simple diagram of the eye of a person who is
 (a) in a dark room;
 (b) walking around in bright sunlight.

(iii) Why might explorers to the Arctic or Antarctic suffer from snow-blindness? How could it be avoided?

People who can see objects close to but can't see distant objects clearly are said to be **shortsighted**. This occurs because the eye lens focuses the rays of light from a distant object *in front of* the retina, so creating a blurred image. This problem can be overcome by wearing glasses or contact lenses.

(iv) What kind of glasses (lenses) should someone who suffers from shortsightedness wear if they are to see clearly? Explain your answer fully using a ray diagram.

Some people suffer from longsightedness, i.e. they can see distant objects but not those close to. This occurs because the eye lens focuses the rays of light from near objects *behind* the retina.

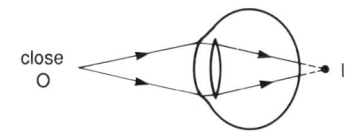

(v) What kind of glasses (lenses) should someone who suffers from longsightedness wear if they are to see clearly? Explain your answer fully using a ray diagram.

100 *Waves*

2 Which type of mirrors might be used in the situations described below? Give reasons for your choice.

   (i) a mirror in a tailor's shop
   (ii) a make-up or shaving mirror
   (iii) a mirror positioned at a sharp bend to enable approaching traffic to see around it
   (iv) the tiny mirror used by dentists to inspect your teeth
   (v) the mirror used at the back of a search light

3 Explain why we sometimes see vehicles on the road with ƎƆИAJUᙠMA written on them.

4 Explain the difference between transverse and longitudinal waves. Give one example of each type of wave.

5 (i) Draw a diagram of a wave. Label both its amplitude and its wave length.
   (ii) Your diagram represents a sound wave. What would we hear if
       (a) the wavelength got shorter?
       (b) the amplitude got larger?
       (c) the shape of the wave changed?

6 If a tuning fork of frequency 250 Hz produces a sound wave 1.2 m long, what is the speed of sound?

7 (i) What is meant by the word 'supersonic' in the phrase 'supersonic aircraft'?
   (ii) What is meant by the word 'ultrasonic' in the phrase 'ultrasonic dog whistle'?
   (iii) Noise pollution is a real problem for people who have to work with very noise machinery. Suggest one way in which they could overcome this problem.

8 Copy this table of the electromagnetic spectrum and fill in the blank spaces.

Type of wave	X-rays				Micro-waves	
			3×10^8 m/s			
				sense of feel or touch		
					microwave oven	

(i) What property of these waves increases as we move from left to right in this table?
(ii) What property of these waves increases as we move from right to left in this table?
(iii) Name five properties or characteristics that these waves have in common.

9 A ship searching for fish emits sound waves which are reflected from the sea-bed. If the speed of sound in water is known and the time that elapses before the echo is heard is measured, it is possible to calculate how deep the water is at that point.
(i) What will the operator hear if a shoal of fish swims under the ship? How could the operator very roughly assess how deep the shoal is?
(ii) Suggestion one way in which the detector might be receiving a false signal (i.e. there are no fish below).
(iii) If sound waves travel through water at 1500 m/s,
  (a) how deep is the sea-bed if an echo is heard after 1 s?
  (b) how quickly is an echo heard if a shoal of fish swims 250 m below the ship?

Electrostatic spraying

The most efficient way to paint the body of a car is to use an electrostatic spray gun. This not only produces small droplets of paint but also electrostatically charges them as they emerge from the nozzle. Because each droplet has the same charge they repel, so ensuring that the mist remains fine and no large droplets form.

The car being sprayed is given the opposite charge. It attracts the droplets, this therefore wastes less paint, as well as ensuring that all surfaces receive a good coating.

Electrostatic precipitation

In order to reduce air pollution, most heavy industries now install electrostatic precipitators in their chimneys.

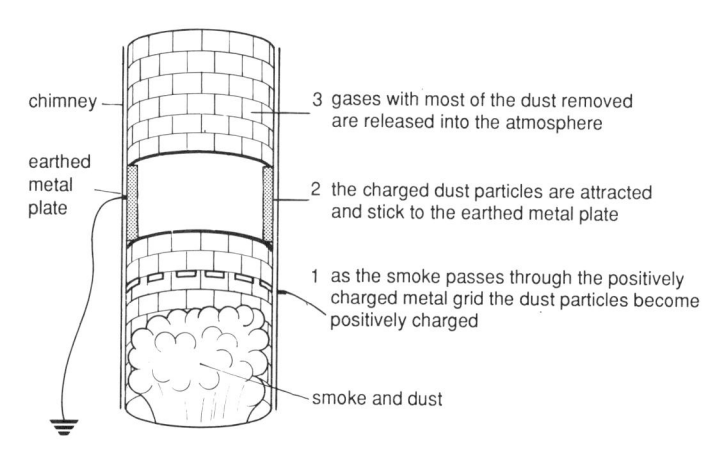

- chimney
- earthed metal plate
- 3 gases with most of the dust removed are released into the atmosphere
- 2 the charged dust particles are attracted and stick to the earthed metal plate
- 1 as the smoke passes through the positively charged metal grid the dust particles become positively charged
- smoke and dust

Conductors and insulators

Static electricity cannot be produced by rubbing just any two objects together. The objects must be made of materials which hold on to the charges produced by friction and do not allow them to escape.

Materials which do not hold on to the charges produced by friction but allow them to flow away are called **conductors.**

Materials which do hold on to the charges produced by friction are called **insulators.**

ELECTRICITY AND MAGNETISM
6.1 Static electricity

6

If you comb your hair and then hold the comb close to some small pieces of paper they will probably jump up and stick to the comb. If you take off a nylon blouse or shirt you will often notice that it tries to stick to your body. These things happen because of the presence of **static electricity.**

Static electricity can be produced by friction. If, for example, we rub a piece of plastic such as a polythene rod with a duster, then both objects become charged.

Before being rubbed, the duster and the polythene rod contain equal numbers of positive and negative charges, i.e. they are neutral or uncharged. When they are rubbed together the rod steals some negative charges (more usually called electrons) from the duster. The rod is now, therefore, negatively charged and the duster, which has too few electrons, is positively charged.

Attraction and repulsion

If two objects which are similarly charged are placed near each other they will repel.

If two objects which are oppositely charged are placed near each other they will attract.

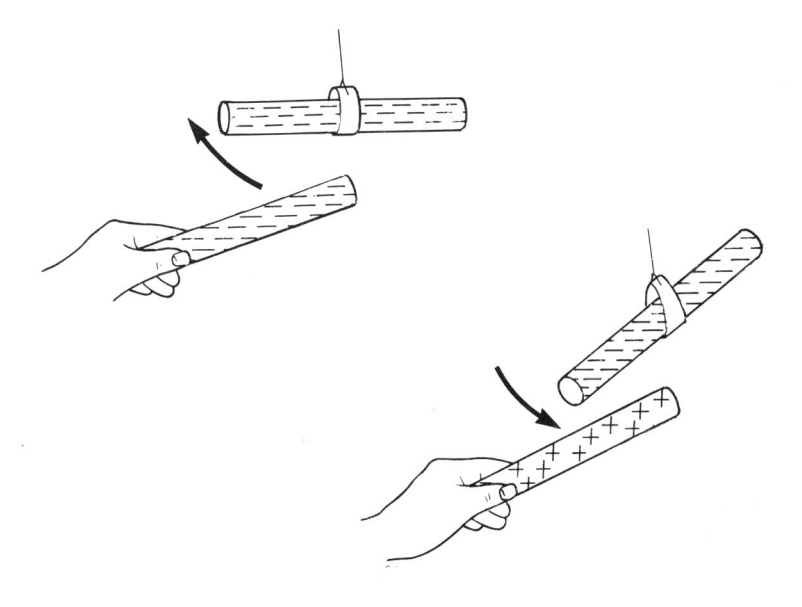

ELECTRICITY AND MAGNETISM
6.2 Electric current

Without electricity the world we live in would be a very different place. There would be no electric lights, no electric fires, no television, no radio, no telephone, etc. Nowadays, although we can't see them, electric currents are never far away.

Electric current is the movement or flow of charge. In metals such as a piece of copper wire, it is the negative charges, i.e. the electrons which move.

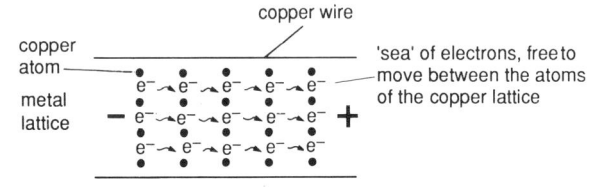

When a **cell** is connected to form a complete circuit, it pumps electrons from its negative terminal through the wires and back to its positive terminal.

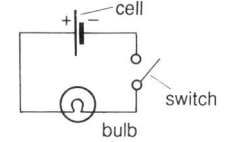

Incomplete circuit – no flow of charge.

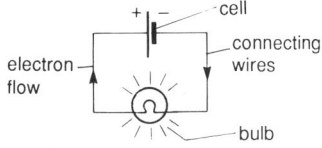

Complete circuit – charge flows – the bulb is lit.

Q What is happening to the circuit in this torch when the button is
(a) pressed,
(b) released?

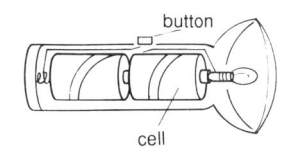

If several cells are connected together the combination is called a **battery.**

Electricity and magnetism 105

When the torch is turned on, the electrons flow along just one path – from the battery through the bulb and back to the battery. However, when a hi-fi system is being used the electrons may flow along several different routes, e.g. through the amplifier or through the cassette player or through the radio.

Circuits like the torch which contain no branches are called **series circuits.**

Circuits like that of the hi-fi system which contain branches are called **parallel circuits.**

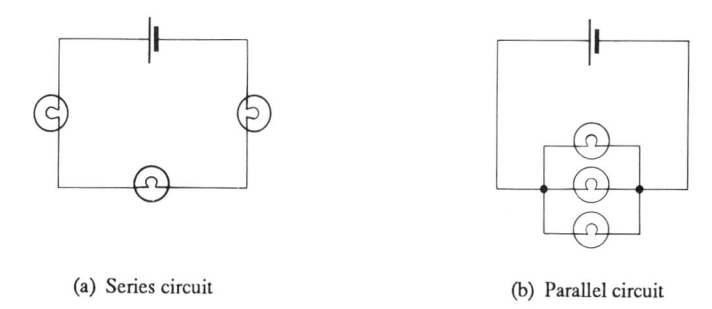

(a) Series circuit   (b) Parallel circuit

Electron flow and conventional current

When scientists first experimented with current electricity, they did not know which type of charge was flowing around the circuit. They guessed incorrectly that the charges were positive and they therefore assumed that electric current flowed from the positive to the negative.

Even though we now know this is incorrect, it has been agreed by all scientists to continue to think of electric current as flowing from the positive to the negative. This is called **conventional current.**

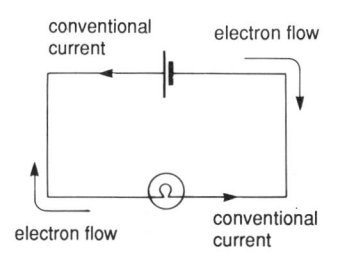

From now on all the currents in this book will be conventional currents.

Electric charge

We measure electric charge in units called **coulombs** (C). 1 C of charge is equivalent to the charge stored on approximately six million, million, million electrons. As you can see from this, the amount of charge carried by one electron is very, very small.

Electric current

We measure the size of an electric current in **amperes** (A). This tells us the number of coulombs of charge which flow past a particular point in the circuit each second.

If 5 C of charge flow past point P in 1 s then the current flowing in the circuit is 5 A.

If 10 C of charge flow past point P in 1 s then the current flowing in the circuit is 10 A.

If 6 C of charge flow past point P in 2 s then the current flowing in the circuit is 3 A.

We can calculate the current flowing in a circuit using the equation

$$\text{current} = \frac{\text{charge}}{\text{time}} \quad \text{or} \quad I = \frac{Q}{t}$$

where I = current
Q = charge
t = time

Example

If 20 C of charge flow through a bulb in 10 s, how large is the current in the circuit?

$$I = \frac{Q}{t}$$

$$= \frac{20\,\text{C}}{10\,\text{s}}$$

$$= \underline{\underline{2\ \text{A}}}$$

Measuring current in series and parallel circuits

We measure the current flowing in a circuit using an instrument called an **ammeter.** This is connected in series with the part of the circuit we are studying.

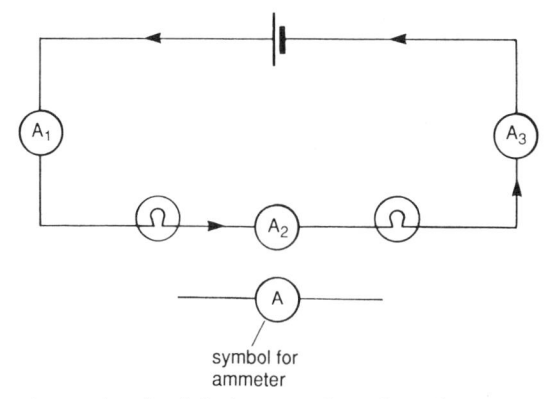

symbol for ammeter

The current in a series circuit is the same throughout; i.e. ammeters A_1, A_2 and A_3, all give the same reading.

In parallel circuits, the current divides and follows different paths.

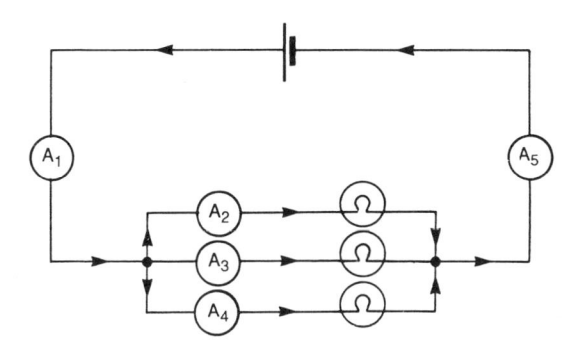

The sum of the currents in the branches of a parallel circuit is equal to the current entering and leaving the network. i.e. The sum of the readings of ammeters A_2, A_3 and A_4 equals the reading of ammeter A_1, which is the same as the reading of A_5.

ELECTRICITY AND MAGNETISM
6.3 Electromotive force and potential difference

6

Electromotive force

In order to move around a circuit, charges need energy. They usually receive this energy from a cell or battery. The amount of energy given to the charges is determined by the **electromotive force** (e.m.f.) of the cell.

This cell has an e.m.f. of 1.5 V because it gives 1.5 J of energy to each coulomb of charge which passes through it.

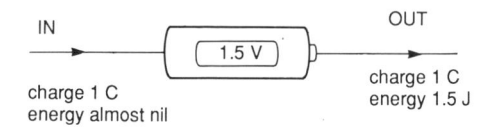

```
        IN                              OUT
        ──▶─┤ 1.5 V ├──▶──
        charge 1 C          charge 1 C
        energy almost nil   energy 1.5 J
```

This cell has an e.m.f. of 9 V because it gives 9 J of energy to each coulomb of charge which passes through it.

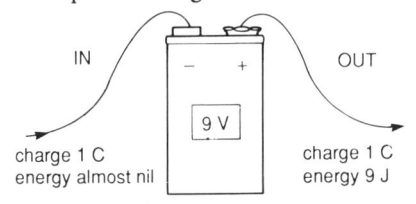

```
        IN            OUT
                − +
              │ 9 V │
        charge 1 C          charge 1 C
        energy almost nil   energy 9 J
```

Potential difference and the voltmeter

As charges move around a circuit, they 'use up' all their energy wending their way through the various components.

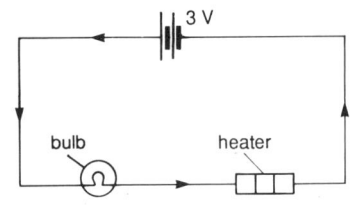

```
              ┤├ 3 V
         ◀────┤├────
        │              │
        │              │
        │  bulb    heater │
        └──(X)────[=]──▶──┘
```

As each coulomb of charge passes through the battery in the circuit above it receives 3 J of energy. As it then passes through the light bulb and heater, nearly all of this energy is used up, i.e it is changed into heat and light energy. In contrast, the charges flow very easily through the connecting wires and use up almost no energy in this part of the circuit.

Electricity and magnetism 109

To discover how much energy is used up as charges flow through the bulb, we use an instrument called a **voltmeter**.

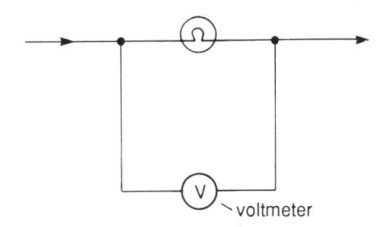

When a voltmeter is connected across a component like this, it is measuring potential difference or p.d. e.g. If the p.d. across the bulb is 2.5 V this means that when one coulomb of charge flows through the bulb, 2.5 J of electrical energy are converted into heat and light energy.

Series circuits

If all the electrical energy received from the cell is converted into other forms of energy in the external part of the circuit, then the sum of the external potential differences is equal to the potential difference across the cell or battery. i.e. the sum of the readings of voltmeters V_1, V_2 and V_3 equals the reading of voltmeter V_c.

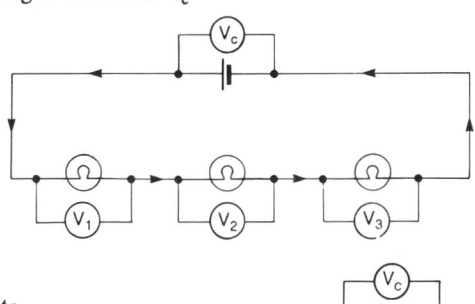

Parallel circuits

In a parallel circuit the potential difference across all branches of the network will be identical. i.e. Voltmeters V_c, V_1, V_2 and V_3, all give the same reading.

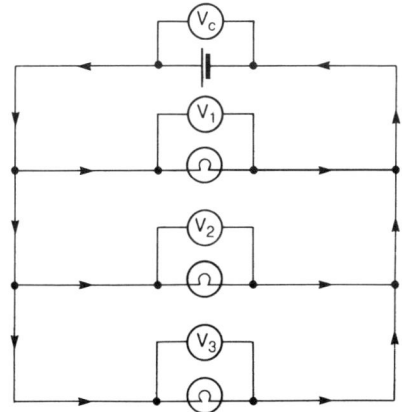

ELECTRICITY AND MAGNETISM
6.4 Resistance

What is electrical resistance?

When electricity flows through a metallic conductor such as a length of copper wire, some of the more loosely held electrons of the wire are travelling between the atoms of the lattice. If the electrons can do this easily, we say that that piece of wire has a low resistance. If, however, the electrons find it difficult, then we say that it has a high resistance.

The resistance of a piece of wire at room temperature depends upon
(a) its length – the longer the wire, the greater its resistance;
(b) its cross-sectional area – the thicker the wire, the smaller its resistance;
(c) the material from which the wire is made.

Using resistance to control current

Many electrical and electronic circuits contain components which could be easily damaged if too large a current flows through them. One way of protecting these components is to include a resistor in these circuits.

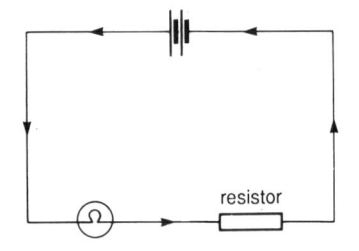

This fixed resistor prevents too large a current from passing through the bulb.

When we adjust the volume or brightness of our TV sets we are altering the size of the currents that flow inside these appliances by using variable resistors.

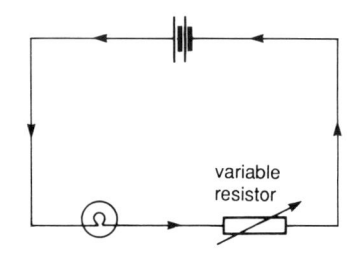

When the resistance of this variable resistor is altered the brightness of the bulb changes. This is a simple dimmer switch circuit, like those used in the cinema or theatre.

The effect of temperature on resistance

(a) Metallic conductors

At room temperature the atoms of a metallic conductor are not stationary but are vibrating gently. These vibrations hinder the passage of the electrons through the wire. If the wire is cooled down, the atomic vibrations decrease and the flow of the electrons is much easier, i.e. the metal has a lower resistance. If, however, the wire is warmed, the atomic vibrations become more violent and the flow of electrons is much more difficult, i.e. the metal has a greater resistance.

(b) Semiconductors

In a semiconductor there are far fewer free electrons than in a metallic conductor. The movement of charge through these materials is therefore quite difficult. If, however, a semiconductor is heated, more electrons become free and the movement of charge is much easier, i.e. the resistance of the material has decreased.

Thermistors are resistors made from a semiconducting material. Small changes in temperature produce large changes in the thermistor's resistance. Thermistors are therefore often used in circuits to detect temperature changes, e.g. fire alarms, thermostats, etc.

ELECTRICITY AND MAGNETISM
6.5 Ohm's Law

If we want to alter the size of the current in a circuit, we can do so in two ways.
(a) We can alter the resistance in the circuit.
(b) We can introduce into the circuit a cell with a larger or smaller e.m.f..

In 1826 a scientist named George Ohm carried out a series of experiments to discover the relationship between the size of a current in a wire and the p.d. across it. The circuit shown here can be used to verify the relationship Ohm discovered.

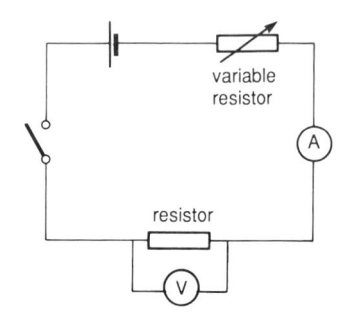

When the switch is closed, the current in the resistor and the p.d. across its ends are noted. The variable resistor is then altered and new values of current and p.d. noted. The experiment is repeated several more times and a table of the results drawn up.

Typical results

V/volts	I/amperes
0.0	0.0
2.0	0.5
4.0	1.0
6.0	1.5
8.0	2.0
10.0	2.5

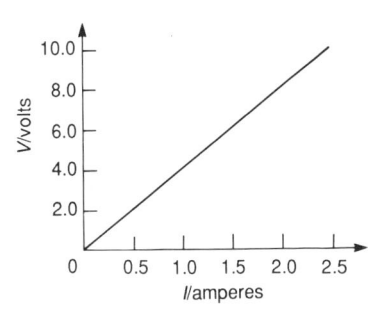

When Ohm carried out his experiments he discovered that for a metallic conductor (e.g. a length of wire) a graph of p.d. against current gave a straight line graph through the origin. He summarised his results in a law.

Ohm's Law

> The current flowing through a resistor is directly proportional to the potential difference across its ends provided that the temperature remains constant.

i.e.
$$V \alpha I$$

or
$$\frac{V}{I} = R \text{ (a constant)}$$

This equation is more usually written as

$$\boxed{V = I \times R}$$

R is a measure of the resistance of the wire in ohms (Ω).

Examples

1 If a current of 1.5 A flows through a wire when a p.d. of 3 V is applied across it what is the resistance of the wire?

$$R = \frac{V}{I}$$
$$= \frac{3 \text{ V}}{1.5 \text{ A}}$$
$$= \underline{\underline{2 \ \Omega}}$$

2 How large a potential difference must be applied across a wire of resistance 20 Ω in order that a current of 0.2 A flows through it?

$$V = IR$$
$$= 0.2 \text{ A} \times 20 \Omega$$
$$= \underline{\underline{4 \text{ V}}}$$

3 How large a current will flow if a p.d. of 12 V is applied across a 4 Ω resistor?

$$V = IR$$
$$I = \frac{V}{R}$$
$$= \frac{12 \text{ V}}{4 \Omega}$$
$$= \underline{\underline{3 \text{ A}}}$$

Ohmic and non-ohmic conductors

Although a graph of p.d. against current for many conductors gives a straight line graph passing through the origin, for some this is not the case. e.g.

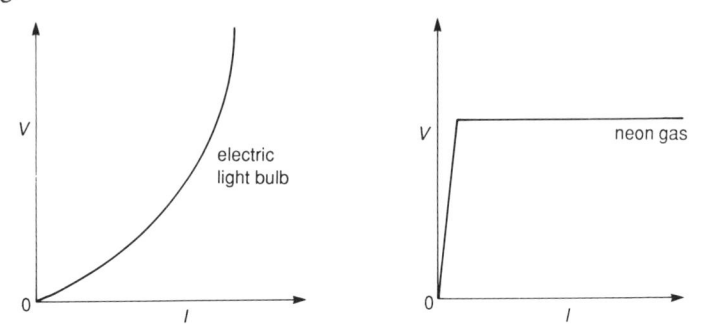

Those conductors which do give a straight line graph through the origin are called **ohmic conductors**. Those that do not are called **non-ohmic conductors**.

In many circuits combinations of resistors are used to control current and voltage.

Connecting resistors in a series

If several resistors are connected in series their total resistance can be found using the equation

$$R_T = r_1 + r_2 + r_3 + ...$$

Example

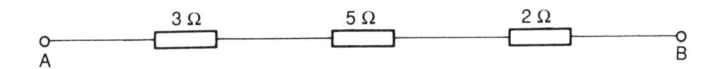

Total resistance between A and B = $3\,\Omega + 5\,\Omega + 2\,\Omega$
$$= \underline{\underline{10\,\Omega}}$$

Connecting resistors in parallel

If several resistors are connected in parallel their total resistance can be found using the equation

$$\frac{1}{R_T} = \frac{1}{r_1} + \frac{1}{r_2} + \frac{1}{r_3} + \ldots$$

Example

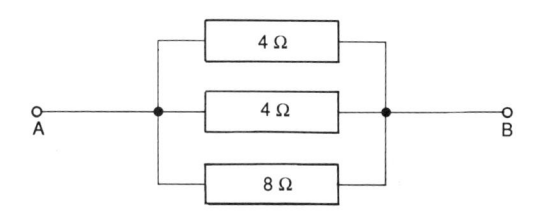

$$\frac{1}{R_T} = \frac{1}{4\,\Omega} + \frac{1}{4\,\Omega} + \frac{1}{8\,\Omega}$$

$$= \frac{5}{8}\,\Omega$$

$$\therefore R_T = \frac{8}{5}\,\Omega$$

$$= \underline{\underline{1.6\ \Omega}}$$

ELECTRICITY AND MAGNETISM
6.6 Basic magnetism

6

Magnets and magnetic materials

Magnets have the ability to attract certain metals, e.g. iron, steel, nickel and cobalt. These are called magnetic materials. Materials which are not attracted are called non-magnetic materials and include copper, tin, wood, plastic, etc. Fridges make use of the attractive properties of a magnetic strip to ensure a good seal when the door is closed.

Q Why is it important to keep a fridge door closed tight?

Steel filings produced by the moving parts of car engines can be removed using magnets.

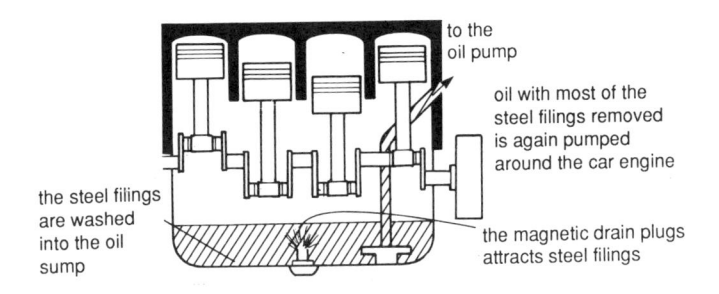

Q What would happen if the steel filings were not removed?
   If on close inspection of a magnetic drain plug a mechanic could see lots of steel filings, what might he conclude about the car engine?

Magnetic materials such as iron filings are strongly attracted to certain parts of the magnet. These are called poles.

If a bar magnet is suspended so that it is free to rotate horizontally, it will come to rest so that its north pole is pointing northwards and its south pole pointing southwards, i.e. it is behaving like a simple compass.

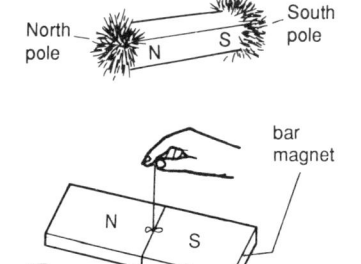

If two unlike poles are placed close together they attract.

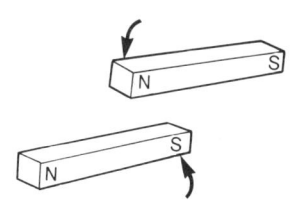

If two similar poles are placed close together they repel.

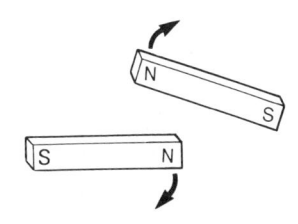

Q How do Maglev (magnetic levitation) trains make use of magnetic repulsion?

Magnetic fields

Around a magnetised object such as a bar magnet there is a volume of space where we can detect magnetism. This space is called a magnetic field. We can discover the shape of a magnetic field using iron filings or plotting compasses.

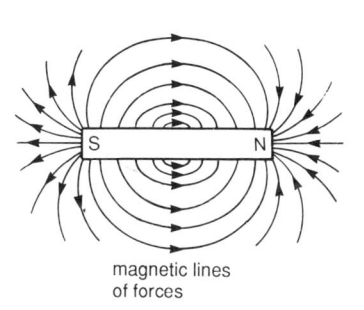

magnetic lines of forces

Magnetic lines of force:

(a) show the shape of the magnetic field;
(b) show the strength of the magnetic field (the field is strongest where the lines are closest together);
(c) always travel from the north pole of a magnet to the south pole.

ELECTRICITY AND MAGNETISM
6.7 Electromagnetism

In 1819 a Danish physicist named Oersted accidentally discovered that an electric current passing through a wire created a magnetic field around it. The magnetic field is cylindrical in shape, centred on the wire, and is strongest close to the wire. If the direction of the current in the wire is reversed so too is the direction of the magnetic field.

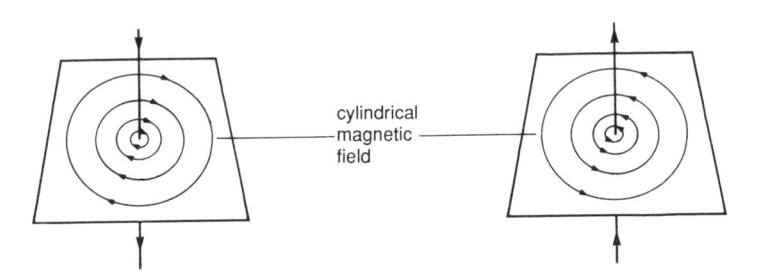

cylindrical magnetic field

The direction of magnetic field created by a current can be found using **Maxwell's corkscrew rule.**

Imagine you are holding a corkscrew or screwdriver in your hand. Decide which way (clockwise or anti-clockwise) you need to turn the screw so that it moves in the same direction the current is flowing. Whichever direction you turn the screw, that is the direction of the magnetic field

direction of rotation (field)

direction of movement (current)

If we wrap a piece of wire around and through a card to make a coil as shown here, the magnetic fields produced by each wire overlap and reinforce each other, creating a very strong magnetic field. The shape of the magnetic field is the same as that produced by a strong bar magnet. This field, however, can be turned on and off, made stronger or weaker, or its polarity changed.

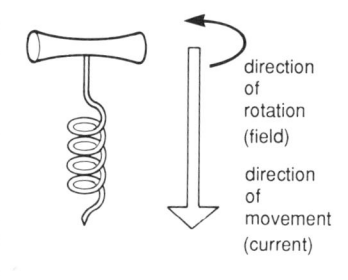

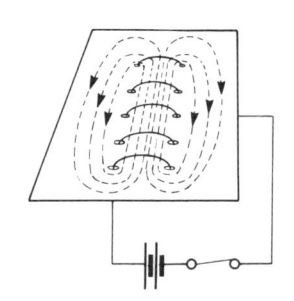

The polarity of the magnetic field can be determined by looking at one end of the coil and deciding which way the current flows around it. If it is clockwise, a south pole will be produced. If it is anticlockwise a north pole will be produced.

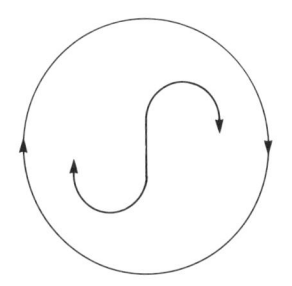

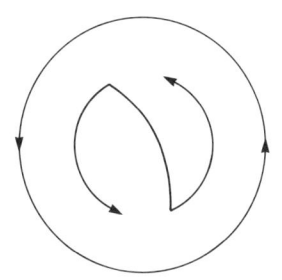

The main factors which determine the strength of the magnetic field produced by a coil or **solenoid** are:

(a) the number of turns on the coil;
(b) the size of the current flowing through the coil;
(c) the concentration or density of the magnetic lines of force – if the coil is wrapped around a piece of iron the iron becomes magnetised and concentrates the magnetic field around it.

Electromagnets

In a scrapyard, picking up and dropping old cars wouldn't be possible using a permanent magnet but it can be done using an electromagnet.

When current passes through the solenoid of an electromagnet the soft iron core it is wrapped around becomes strongly magnetised and so can be used to pick up a car. When the current is turned off the iron core loses all its magnetism and so the car can be dropped. Materials such as iron which are easily magnetised and demagnetised are said to be **magnetically soft.**

If a **magnetically hard** material such as steel were used instead, it would retain its magnetism when the current was turned off and therefore would not be an appropriate material to use for the core of an electromagnet.

120 *Electricity and magnetism*

Uses of electromagnets

Electric bell

When the bell push is pressed the circuit is complete and current flows. The soft iron cores become magnetised and attract the iron armature. As the hammer strikes the bell the armature pulls away from the contact screw. The circuit is broken, the current no longer flows and therefore the cores are no longer magnetised. The armature is pulled back to its original position by a spring and the circuit is once more complete. The whole process can now begin again and will continue as long as the bell push is pressed.

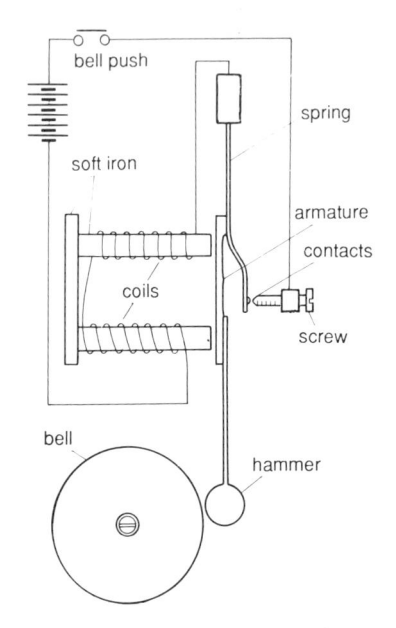

Q A circuit such as this is known as a make and break circuit. Why?

Door chimes

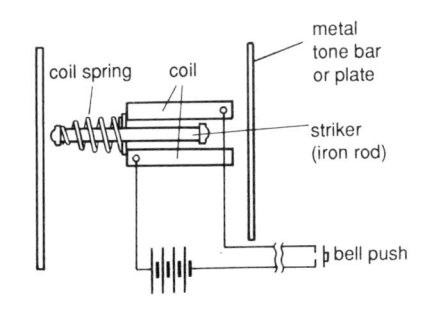

When the bell push is pressed a magnetic field is created in and around the coil. This field pulls the rod into the coil, causing it to strike the right hand tone bar whilst at the same time compressing the spring. When the bell push is released the magnetic field collapses and the compressed spring drives the rod back into the left hand tone bar.

Electricity and magnetism 121

Relays

Sometimes we may wish to control the current flowing in one circuit by using a second separate circuit. This is particularly true if the current flowing in the second circuit is very large and therefore possibly dangerous. A device which enables us to do this is called a **relay**.

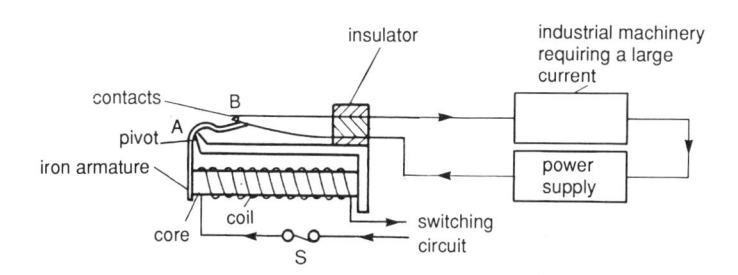

When the switch S is closed current flows through the wire wrapped around the soft iron core. The core therefore becomes magnetised and attracts the iron armature. The armature pivots around point A and in doing so pushes the contacts at B together so that the secondary circuit is complete. If the switch is opened the armature is released, the contacts spring apart and current ceases to flow in the secondary circuit.

Telephone earpiece

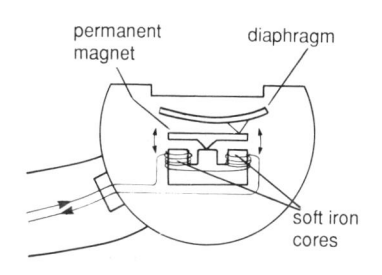

A varying current originating from the mouthpiece of a second telephone flows around the soft iron cores. This creates a varying magnetic field which causes the permanent magnet and the iron diaphragm to vibrate. Sound waves similar to those entering the mouthpiece are therefore produced by the earpiece.

ELECRICITY AND MAGNETISM
6.8 Force on a current-carrying conductor in a magnetic field   6

As we have seen, a current flowing through a wire creates around it a magnetic field. If this wire is placed between the poles of a permanent magnet the two magnetic fields will overlap and interact with each other. This interaction causes the wire to move.

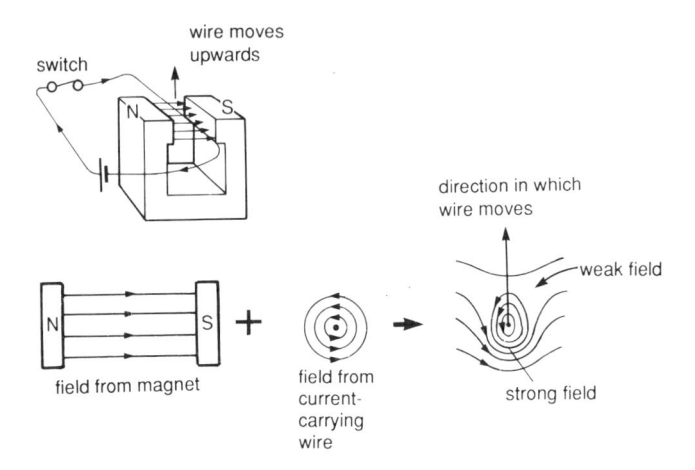

If either the direction of the current in the wire, or the direction of the magnetic field from the permanent magnet is reversed, then the wire experiences a force in the opposite direction.

Fleming's Left Hand Rule

An easy way to work out the direction in which the wire will move is to use Fleming's Left Hand Rule.

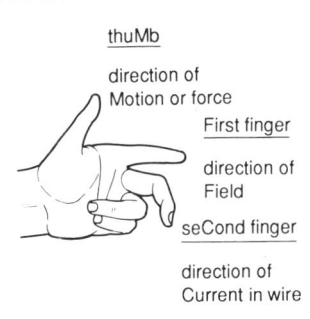

thuMb
direction of Motion or force

First finger
direction of Field

seCond finger
direction of Current in wire

Coil in a magnetic field

If we place two pieces of wire between the poles of a magnet and then pass a current through each, but in opposite directions, one wire will feel a force trying to push it upwards while the second wire will feel a force trying to push it downwards. If the two wires are opposite sides of a coil of wire, the coil will rotate. This is the basic principle of an electric motor.

Remember, when you show the direction in which a current is flowing

⊙ is the symbol for current flowing out of the paper;
⊗ is the symbol for current flowing into the paper.

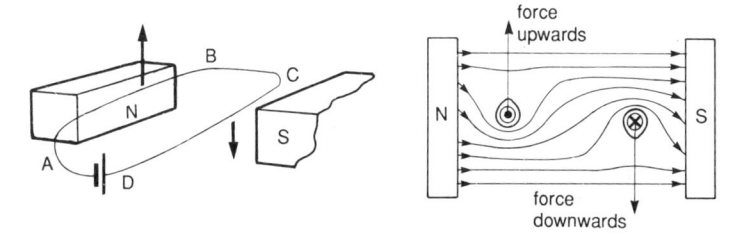

Resultant magnetic field

Electric motor

If a coil is to rotate continuously the direction of the forces on the wires must change continuously, e.g. wire AB must first be pushed up and then down, and then up and then down, etc. We can do this by changing the direction of the current in the wires using a commutator attached as shown in (a).

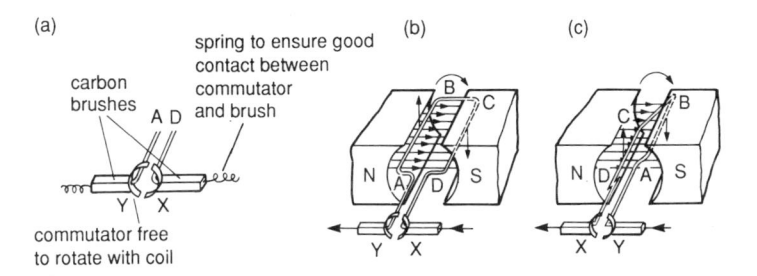

If X is connected to the positive terminal of the cell, current will flow around the coil in direction DCBA. The coil will experience forces causing it to rotate clockwise as shown in (b).

As the coil approaches the vertical position its momentum causes the rotation to continue until X is connected to the negative terminal of the cell. Current now passes around the coil in the opposite direction and so AB moves downwards and CD upwards as shown in (c).

When the coil again reaches the vertical position, the direction of the current changes again and so the coil continues to rotate.

In real electric motors it is important that the turning motion is smooth and not jerky. To achieve this, several coils are put together. Also the permanent magnets of the simple motor are replaced by curved electromagnets.

Moving coil meter

When current passes through the coil it rotates. As it does so it is opposed by the two springs. The amount by which the coil is able to rotate reflects the size of the current.

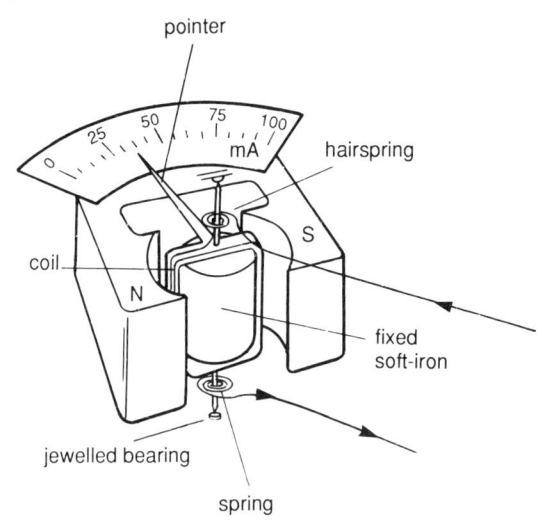

Moving coil loudspeaker

The electrical signals from a microphone or radio are in the form of an electric current which is continuously changing direction. If these signals are fed into the coil situated between the poles of the permanent magnet it will be made to vibrate back and forth. This in turn will cause the cone to vibrate, so producing the sound waves we hear.

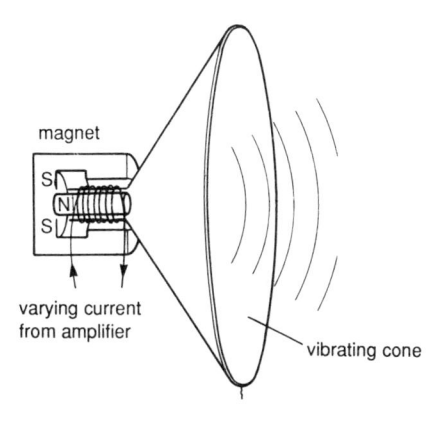

ELECTRICITY AND MAGNETISM
6.9 Electromagnetic induction

6

On p.123 we saw that the combination of an electric current and a magnetic field could produce motion (motor principle). The experiments below demonstrate that it is possible to generate an electric current by combining a magnetic field and a moving conductor.

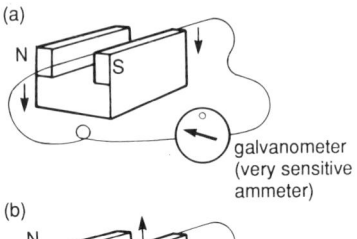

(a) When the wire is moving downwards quickly, there is a large deflection on the galvanometer needle showing that there is current flowing in the circuit.

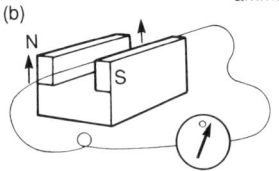

galvanometer (very sensitive ammeter)

(b) When the wire is moving upwards slowly, there is a smaller deflection on the galvanometer needle in the opposite direction.

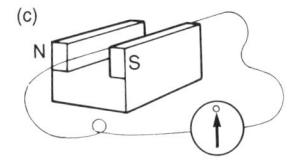

(c) When the wire is held stationary, there is no deflection.

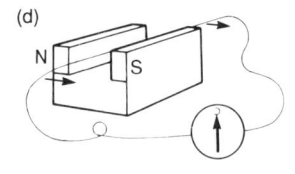

(d) When the wire is moving horizontally, between the poles of the magnet, there is no deflection.

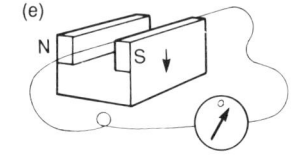

(e) When the wire is held stationary and the magnet moved, there is a deflection.

Electricity and magnetism

Similarly, if a magnet is moved in and out of a coil, current can be generated.

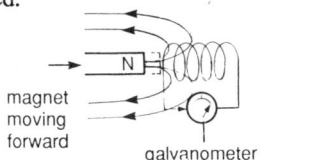

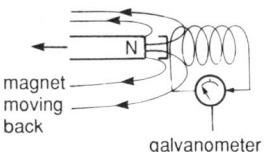

From these experiments we can see that
(a) If a conductor such as a wire moves through a magnetic field, cutting magnetic lines of force, a voltage or e.m.f. is induced across it. The process which produces the e.m.f. is called **electromagnetic induction**. If the wire is part of a complete circuit the e.m.f. induces a current in the wire.
(b) If a conductor is held stationary within a magnetic field or is moved parallel to the magnetic lines of force, there is no cutting of the lines and therefore no current is produced.
(c) If a conductor is held stationary and the magnetic field moved, a current can still be generated.
(d) The size of the induced e.m.f. or current depends upon
   (i) the speed of the movement;
   (ii) the number of wires (coils) cutting the magnetic lines of force;
   (iii) the strength of the magnetic field.
(e) The direction in which the induced current flows depends upon the direction of the movement and the direction of the magnetic field.

We can predict the direction of an induced current in an wire using **Fleming's Right Hand Rule**.

ThuMb	Movement of conductor
First finger	Direction of magnetic Field
SeCond finger	Direction of induced Current

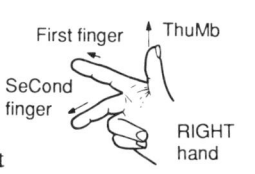

The direction of the current induced in a coil can also be predicted using **Lenz's Law**. This states that 'the induced current flows in a direction such as to oppose the change producing it'.

Pushing a north pole into a coil will induce a current (see the diagram at the top of the page). This current will flow in an anticlockwise direction around the coil, so producing another north pole which tries to push the magnet out.

Pulling the north pole out of a coil produces a clockwise current, i.e. a south pole which tries to prevent the magnet being withdrawn.

ELECTRICITY AND MAGNETISM
6.10 Generators and dynamos

6

If a coil is rotated between the poles of a magnet its wires will cut magnetic lines of force and an induced current will flow. The size and direction of the current change as the position of the coil changes.

(a) When the coil is nearly vertical both sets of wires AB and CD are moving almost parallel to the magnetic lines of force. No lines are being cut by the wires and there is therefore no induced current.

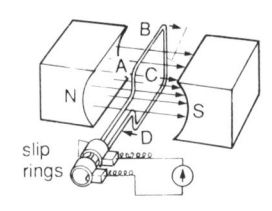

No current.

(b) When the coil is horizontal the wires are moving at right angles to the magnetic lines of force. (AB moving downwards, CD moving upwards.) A large current is therefore induced in the coil.

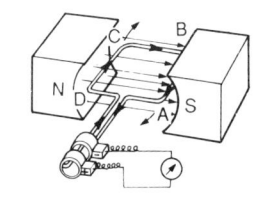

Maximum current.

(c) Again the coil is vertical and so there is no induced current.

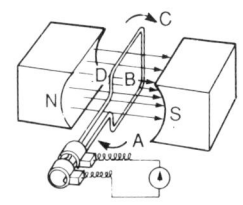

No current.

(d) A large induced current is produced but it flows in the opposite direction to that in (b) (as AB is now moving upwards and CD downwards).

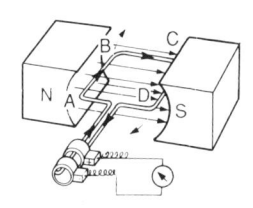

Maximum current but in
the opposite direction to position (b).

Electricity and magnetism 129

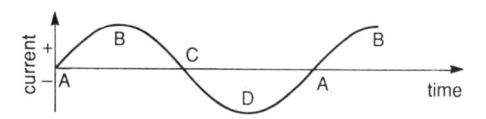

A to A = one complete rotation of coil

A current which flows back and forth like this is called an alternating current (a.c.). The electricity we receive from the Electricity Board is in the form of an alternating current.

Tape recording and playback

(a) The electrical signal from a microphone or hi-fi produces a fluctuating magnetic field around the electromagnet in the recording head. This field produces a pattern of mini magnets on the tape.
(b) When the tape passes the playback head the pattern of mini magnets induces a fluctuating current in the coil. This current is then amplified and fed into loudspeakers or headphones.

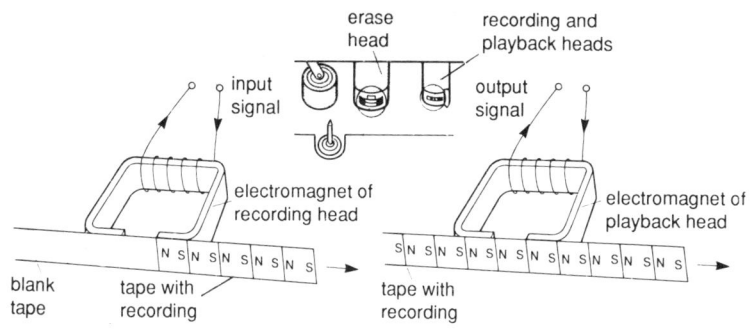

Bicycle dynamo

The knurled knob of this dynamo leans against the side of the bicycle tyre. When the bicycle is ridden the knob turns, causing both the magnet and its field to rotate. As it does so its magnetic lines of force pass through the wires of the coil. The resulting induced current is used to power the bicycle's lights. If the bicycle is stationary no current is induced.

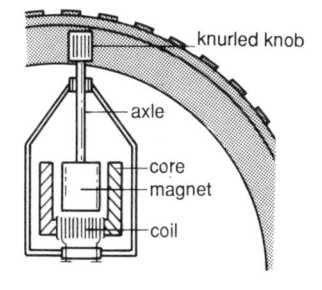

ELECTRICITY AND MAGNETISM
6.11 The transformer

Mutual induction (induction between two coils)

When the switch S is closed current begins to flow around the left circuit. As its value increases from zero, so a magnetic field grows outwards from coil A. As the field grows some of its magnetic lines of force cut through the wires of coil B, inducing a current in it.

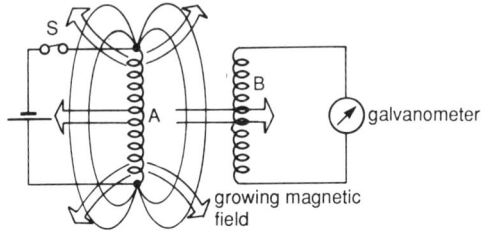

When the switch is opened the field collapses and the magnetic lines of force again cut through the wires of coil B, but this time producing a current in the opposite direction.

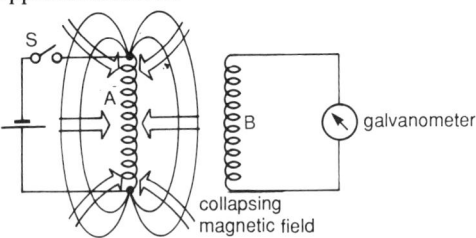

If a soft iron core is placed through the centres of the coils, the size of the induced current increases. This is because the soft iron core increases the magnetic field strength around the two coils. Hence as the field grows and collapses the magnetic lines of force cut through the coils at a greater rate. This combination of two coils linked together by a soft iron core is called a **transformer**.

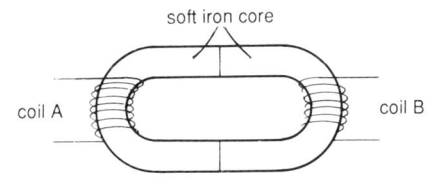

Note: Current is only induced in coil B whilst the current in coil A is *changing*.

Electricity and magnetism 131

Alternating current and the transformer

If an alternating current is fed into coil A (more usually called the **primary coil**), because it is continually changing in size and direction an alternating current of the same frequency in induced in coil B (the **secondary coil**).

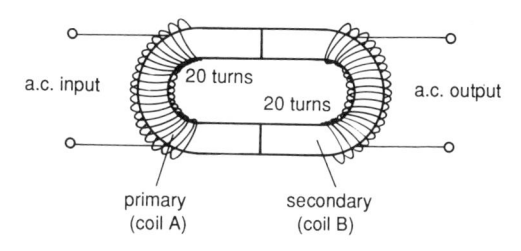

```
a.c. input — [20 turns / 20 turns] — a.c. output
             primary      secondary
             (coil A)     (coil B)
```

In the above circuit the sizes of the alternating currents in the primary and secondary coils, and the induced voltages across the primary and secondary coils, should be the same. However, this is not always the case.

To investigate the input and output voltages of a transformer

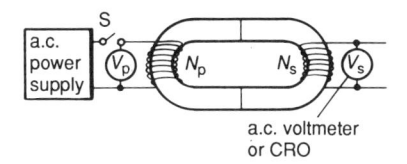

```
a.c. power supply — S — $V_p$ — $N_p$ — $N_s$ — $V_s$ — a.c. voltmeter or CRO
```

1 The numbers of turns on the primary and secondary coils are noted (N_p and N_s).

2 The switch S is closed and the input and output voltages noted (V_p and V_s).

3 The number of turns on either the primary or secondary coil is altered and the voltages again noted.

4 A table showing the values of input and output voltages with the corresponding number of turns on the coils is drawn up.

Typical results

Primary coil		Secondary coil	
No. of turns	Voltmeter reading/V	No. of turns	Voltmeter reading/V
20	12	20	12
20	12	40	24
20	12	60	36
40	12	20	6
40	12	10	3

From this experiment we can see that the size of the induced e.m.f. in the secondary coil depends upon the number of turns on each of the coils and the size of the applied p.d..

The relationship between these four values is shown in the equation below.

$$\frac{\text{number of turns in the primary coil}}{\text{number of turns in the secondary coil}} = \frac{\text{applied voltage}}{\text{induced voltage}}$$

i.e.
$$\boxed{\frac{N_p}{N_s} = \frac{V_p}{V_s}}$$

In practice, the experiment is unlikely to produce results which precisely fit this equation. It is likely that the induced voltage V_s is slightly less than it should be. This is because the equation assumes that the transformer is 100% efficient, i.e. there is no energy loss.

In order to make a transformer as efficient as possible,

(a) the windings on both coils should consist of thick copper wire. This reduces any energy loss due to the heating effect of the current as it passes through the wires.
(b) both coils should be linked with a soft iron core. This increases the magnetic field strength around the coils.
(c) the soft iron core should be laminated (made of thin sheets which are insulated from each other). This minimises any stray currents (eddy currents) which are generated in the core.

Uses of transformers

A transformer is used to increase or decrease alternating voltages which are applied to it. If the output voltage is higher than the input voltage, a step-up transformer is being used. If the output voltage is lower than the input voltage a step-down transformer is being used.

Examples

Many portable cassette recorders require a 9 V supply (9 V battery) to operate correctly. It is possible, however, to operate them using the mains supply, i.e. 240 V a.c.. This is possible because inside the tape recorder there is a small step-down transformer which reduces the mains voltage from 240 V a.c. to 9 V a.c. The alternating current can then be changed to d.c. (rectified) by using a diode (p.150).

One of the most important uses of step-up and step-down transformers is in the National Grid (see Section 6.12). In this system, overhead cables supported by pylons supply the country with electricity which has been generated at the power stations. Voltages of up to 400 000 V are used during transmission but this is reduced in stages to 240 V, using step-down transformers, before the electricity enters our homes.

Calculation

If a p.d. of 12 V a.c. is applied across the terminals of a 50 turn primary coil of a transformer, what will be the output voltage if the number of turns on a secondary coil is (a) 10, (b) 250?

(a) Using

$$\frac{N_p}{N_s} = \frac{V_p}{V_s}$$

$$\therefore V_s = \frac{10}{50} \times 12 \text{V}$$

$$= \underline{\underline{2.4 \text{ V}}}$$

(b) Using

$$\frac{N_p}{N_s} = \frac{V_p}{V_s}$$

$$\therefore V_s = \frac{250}{50} \times 12 \text{V}$$

$$= \underline{\underline{60 \text{ V}}}$$

ELECTRICITY AND MAGNETISM
6.12 Transmission of electricity

6

The electricity which we use in our homes is generated for us at a power station. Here coal, oil, or a nuclear reactor is used to power steam turbines which turn the a.c. generators which make the electrical energy we require.

The diagram below shows what happens to the electricity once it has been generated.

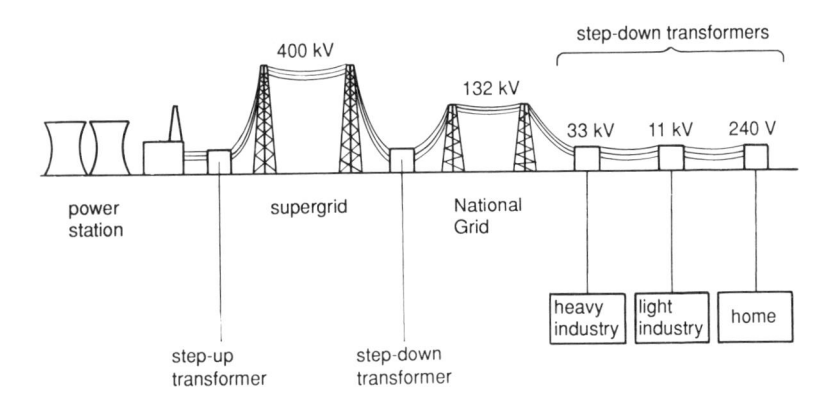

(a) In most power stations electricity is generated at 25 000 V (25 kV).
(b) Step-up transformers then raise the voltage to 400 kV before the electricity is fed into the supergrid.
(c) Close to towns the voltage is reduced by step-down transformers to 132 kV. This reduction allows the cables to be laid underground or to be supported above the ground on smaller pylons.
(d) In the towns, the voltage is further reduced to
    (i)   33 kV which is used by heavy industry;
    (ii) 11 kV which is used by light industry;
    (iii) 240 V which is used in the home.

Q Why do we use a step-up transformer immediately before transmitting the electrical energy and then use a step-down transformer immediately after transmitting it?

Q Why do we transmit alternating current rather than direct current?

The answer to those two questions can be found by setting up the following two circuits.

Electricity and magnetism 135

CIRCUIT 1

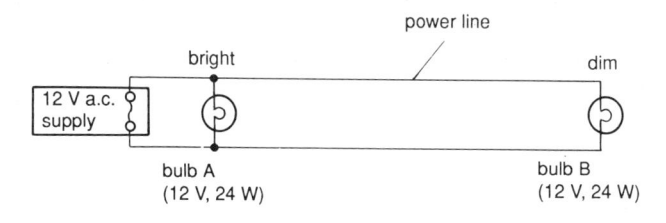

- bulb A (12 V, 24 W): bright
- bulb B (12 V, 24 W): dim
- 12 V a.c. supply, connected via power line

CIRCUIT 2

- bulb A (12 V, 24 W): bright
- bulb B (12 V, 24 W): bright
- 12 V a.c. supply, step-up transformer, power line, step-down transformer

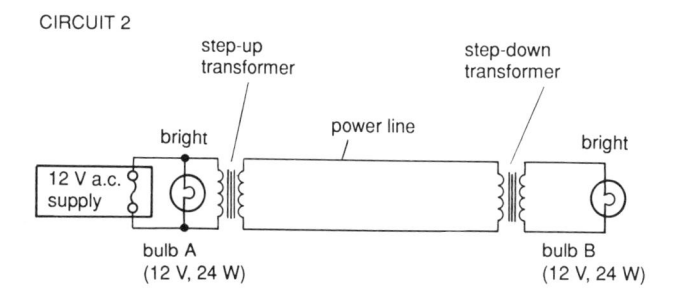

Bulb A, which is connected to the supply before transmission, shows how much energy is being fed into the power line per second.

Bulb B shows us how much energy per second is available for use after transmission.

If the system were 100% efficient, all the energy fed into the power lines should be available for use. However, in circuit 1 bulb B is much dimmer than bulb A, i.e. energy is being lost in the power lines.

Circuit 2 can be seen to be much more efficient, as here bulb A and bulb B are very nearly the same brightness.

From this we can see that when transmitting electrical energy from the power stations to our homes, it is best to use a small current and a high p.d. as less energy is then wasted in heating the power lines.

Note: Although d.c. voltages and currents can be adjusted so that transmission takes place at a high voltage and low current, it is much easier and much more efficient to alter a.c. currents and voltages by using transformers.

ELECTRICITY AND MAGNETISM
6.13 Electrical power

As we have already seen (Section 6.3), when current flows through an appliance electrical energy is changed into other forms of energy. For example, an electric fire converts electrical energy into heat and light energy, and a television converts electrical energy into light and sound energy.

What is a watt?

Electric light bulbs often have two numbers printed upon them.

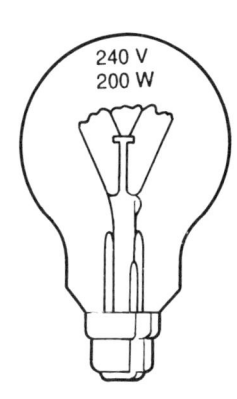

240 V – The first number tells us that when 1 coulomb of charge passes through each bulb 240 joules of electrical energy will be converted into heat and light energy. The second number (60 W or 200 W in our examples) tells us how quickly this energy conversion takes place.

A 60 W bulb changes 60 J of electrical energy into heat and light energy every second.

A 200 W bulb changes 200 J of electrical energy into heat and light energy every second.

When we are looking at how rapidly a piece of apparatus is using energy, we are considering its **power**. We measure power in joules per second or **watts**.

$$1 W = 1 J/s$$

Power rating

We can find the power rating of any appliance provided we know the p.d. across it and the current flowing through it, by using the equation:

$$\text{power} = \text{p.d.} \times \text{current}$$
$$P = V \times I$$

or watts = volts × amperes

Example

When all three bars of an electric fire are turned on, a current of 12.5 A flows through it. If the p.d. across the fire is 240 V, what is the power rating of the fire?

$$P = V \times I$$
$$= 240 \text{ V} \times 12.5 \text{ A}$$
$$= \underline{\underline{3000 \text{ W or 3 kW}}}$$

Typical power ratings

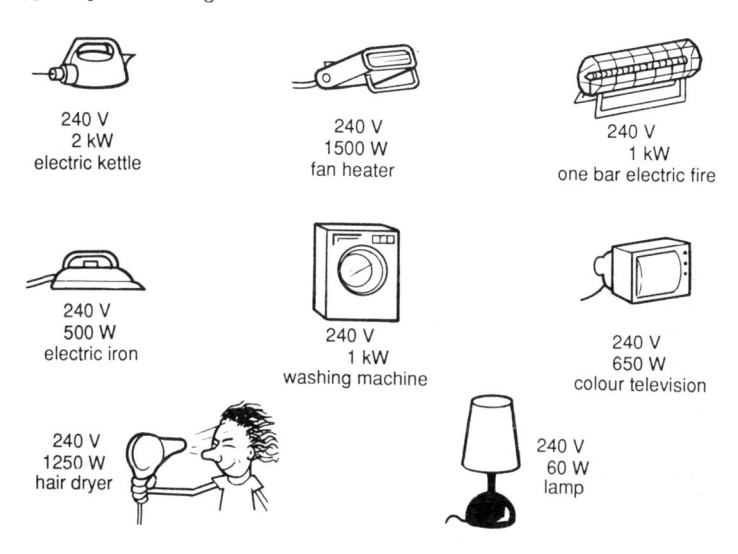

240 V
2 kW
electric kettle

240 V
1500 W
fan heater

240 V
1 kW
one bar electric fire

240 V
500 W
electric iron

240 V
1 kW
washing machine

240 V
650 W
colour television

240 V
1250 W
hair dryer

240 V
60 W
lamp

138 *Electricity and magnetism*

How much energy have I used?

The power rating (or wattage) of an appliance tells us how much energy is being used by the appliance per second. To find the *total* energy used we multiply this figure by the number of seconds the appliance is turned on for.

i.e. $\boxed{\text{energy used} = P \times t \text{ or } V \times I \times t}$

(where t is the time in seconds)

Example

A 60 W electric light bulb is turned on for four hours. How much electrical energy does it convert into heat and light?

Energy used $= P \times t$ (time in seconds)
$= 60 \times 4 \times 60 \times 60$
$= 846\,000\,\text{J or } 864\,\text{kJ}$

Paying for domestic electricity

In our homes we use electrical energy to cook with, to provide us with heat and light, etc. We then have to pay our local Electricity Board for all the energy we have used. We can see from the above example that if we measured the amount of electrical energy we used each year in the home in joules it would be a very, very large number – far too large and clumsy to be of any use. The Electricity Boards therefore measure their energies in much larger quantities called **units**.

Example

If a 1 kW fire is turned on for 1 hour, the amount of energy it would use would be 1 unit. (Sometimes called one **kilowatt hour.**)
  If a 1 kW fire is turned on for 5 hours, the amount of energy it would use would be 5 units.
  If a 3 kW fire is turned on for 5 hours, it would use up 15 units.

i.e. $\boxed{\text{the number of units used} = \text{the wattage of the appliance in kilowatts} \times \text{the time in hours.}}$

Power in transformers

On p. 135 we saw that by using a step-up transformer it was possible to change an input of 12 V a.c. into an output of 240 V a.c. At first it may seem that we are gaining energy but this is not the case. Although the output *voltage* has increased considerably the output *current* has actually decreased.

Example

If a transformer is 100% efficient, then

> energy entering the transformer = energy leaving the transformer

i.e.
$$V_p \times I_p \times t = V_s \times I_s \times t$$
$$V_p \times I_p = V_s \times I_s$$

If the current in the primary coil is 1 A, then

$$12 \text{V} \times 1 \text{ A} = 240 \text{ V} \times I_s$$
$$I_s = \frac{1}{20} \text{ A}$$

i.e. The output voltage has increased by a factor of 20 but the output current has decreased by a factor of 20.

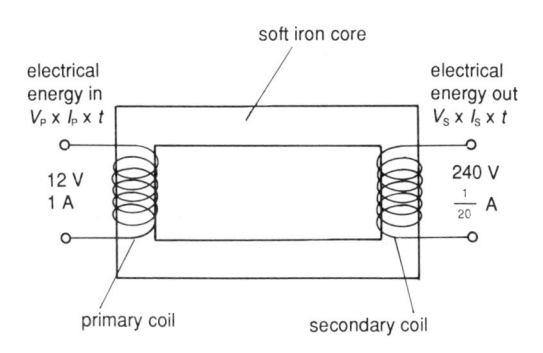

100% efficient transformer

ELECTRICITY AND MAGNETISM
6.14 Electricity in the home

6

The electrical energy generated at the power stations usually enters our homes through underground cables. Immediately it enters a house it is fed via the electricity meter into a box similar to that shown here. This is known as the consumer box. It contains fuses for each of the circuits in the house and a switch which enables us to turn off all the electricity in the house.

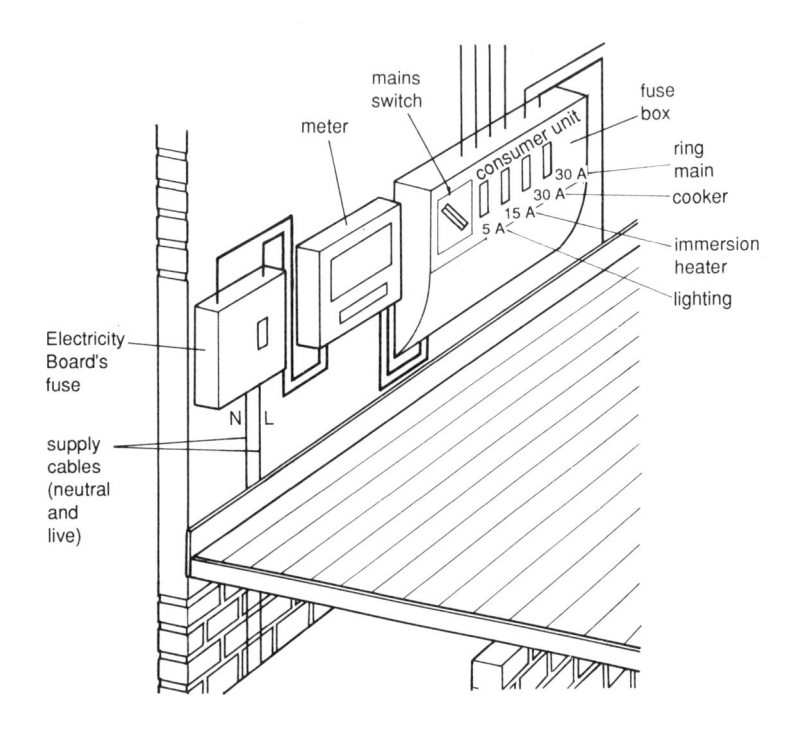

The supply cable entering the house contains two wires, the live wire (L) and the neutral wire (N). The electrical energy we use enters our homes through the live wire whilst the neutral wire completes the circuit.

In the consumer box the supply is divided between several separate circuits. One such circuit is the lighting circuit. This supplies electrical energy to all parts of the house where there are filament bulbs or fluorescent lights.

Electricity and magnetism 141

Ring circuits

Our television sets and stereo systems, etc., receive their electrical energy from a second separate type of circuit called a **ring main**. In this circuit three wires, the live, neutral and earth, run around the rooms of a house in a ring as shown here. Sockets are then connected to these wires in parallel.

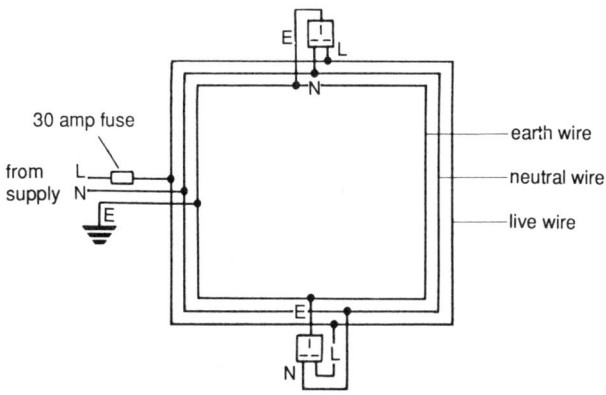

Ring circuit

The earth wire

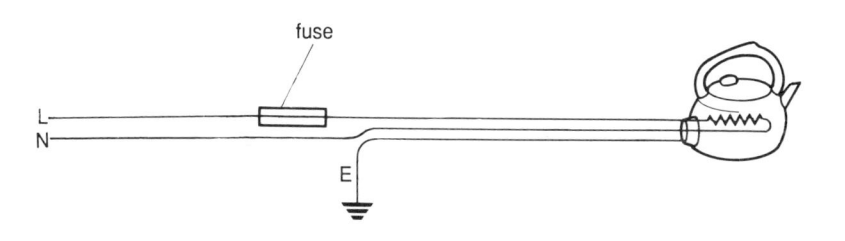

The earth wire is included in a circuit to protect us from receiving an electric shock should an appliance become faulty.

The electric kettle shown here is in good working order. When it is turned on electrical energy will travel through the live wire into the heating element and the circuit is completed by the neutral wire.

142 *Electricity and magnetism*

This electric kettle is not in good working order and it will give an electric shock to anyone who touches it. The live wire which leads the electrical energy into the kettle is broken and is touching the body of the kettle. Electrical energy will flow to earth through the user rather than through the neutral wire and there is therefore a danger of electrocution.

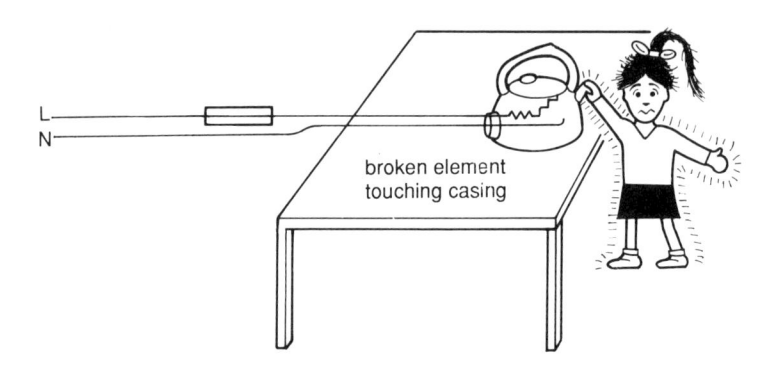

The electric kettle shown below is also faulty, but it is not as dangerous as the kettle in the previous diagram. Because the earth wire is connected to the outer casing, electrical energy from the broken live wire passes to earth through it rather than through the body of the user. The fuse blows, so isolating the kettle.

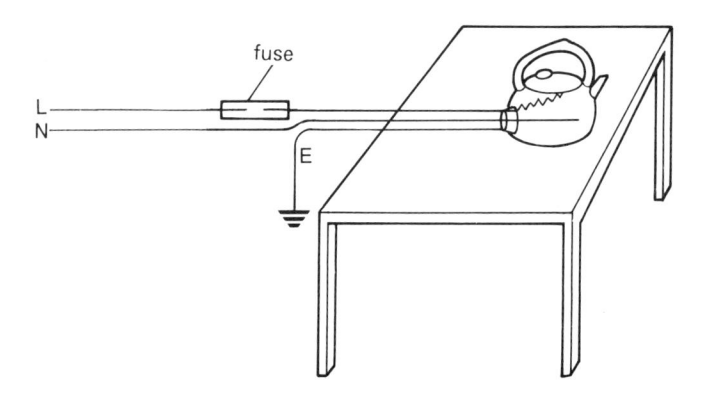

Electricity and magnetism 143

Switches

Switches in the home must always be connected in series with the live wire. This means that when the switch is open the path by which energy enters an appliance has been broken.

If a switch is connected into the neutral wire, only the return path is broken and anyone coming into contact with any of the circuits of the appliance could still receive an electric shock as they themselves become the return circuit. To isolate (completely turn off) an appliance its ON/OFF switch must be included in the *live* wire.

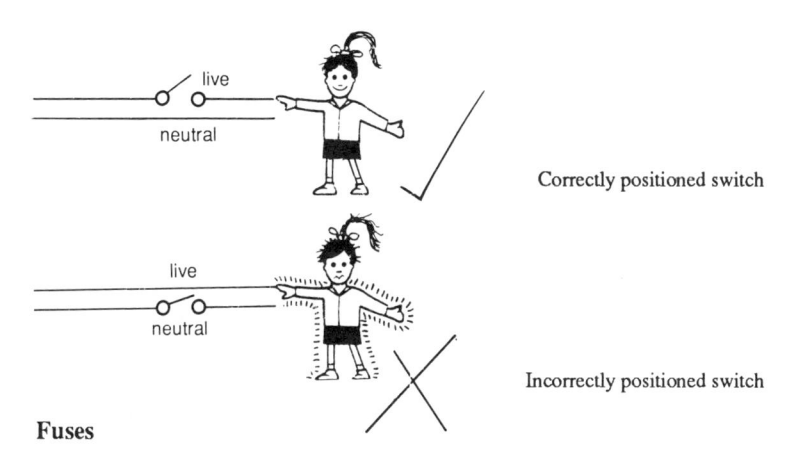

Correctly positioned switch

Incorrectly positioned switch

Fuses

If an appliance or one of its circuits becomes faulty there is a danger that too large a current will flow through the wires. The heating effect of such a current could damage the appliance and possibly set it on fire. To avoid this problem **fuses** are included in all household circuits

The most common household fuses consist of a thin piece of wire enclosed in a plastic cylinder. If too much current passes through the wire it melts, so breaking the circuit. The maximum current a fuse will allow to pass through it depends upon the metal from which the wire is made and its thickness (cross-sectional area). The most common fuses are rated at 1 A, 3 A and 13 A.

Some modern fuses are in the form of a trip switch. When the current exceeds a certain value the switch automatically opens. Once the fault in the circuit has been corrected, the fuse is simply reset (usually by pushing a button). There is no need to replace the whole fuse.

The correct fuse to fit into a circuit is one which melts or trips when a current slightly larger than the one you require flows through it.

Examples

1 A hi-fi has a current of 0.5 A flowing through it. The correct fuse to use in this circuit is the 1 A fuse.

2 A small electric drill has a current of 1.5 A flowing through it. The correct fuse to use in this circuit is the 3 A fuse. A 13 A fuse would allow too high a current to flow in the circuit whilst a 1 A fuse would prevent the correct current (1.5 A) from flowing.

3

Appliance	Typical fuse
Electric fire	13 A
Electric kettle	13 A
Television	3 A
Table lamp	3 A

Earth-leakage circuit breakers (ELCB)

Mains electricity can be lethal. If for example a gardener cuts through the mains cable with her mower, there is a real danger of her receiving a severe electric shock. One way to reduce this danger is to use an **earth-leakage circuit breaker (ELCB).**

ELCBs compare the current flowing into a circuit with that flowing back to the mains. If the incoming current is greater than that leaving (this would be the case if the cable was cut in the above example) the ELCB will instantly cut off the current.

Electricity and magnetism 145

Plugs

To avoid accidents when we connect appliances to mains circuits, we do not use loose wires or crocodile clips but plugs. Great care must be taken to ensure that the wires in a plug are connected to the correct pins.

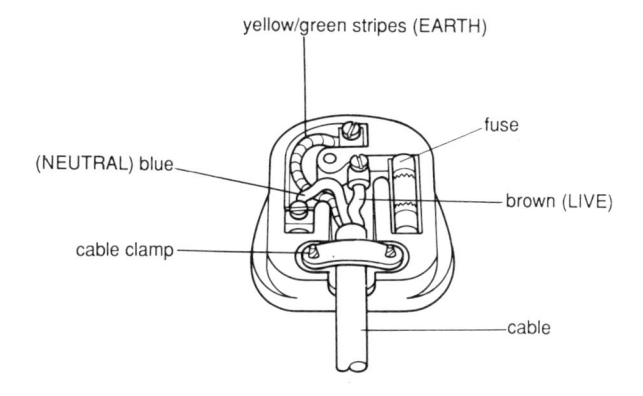

ELECTRICITY AND MAGNETISM
6.15 Questions

1 Two families A and B each bought a set of Christmas tree lights and assembled them according to the instructions enclosed.

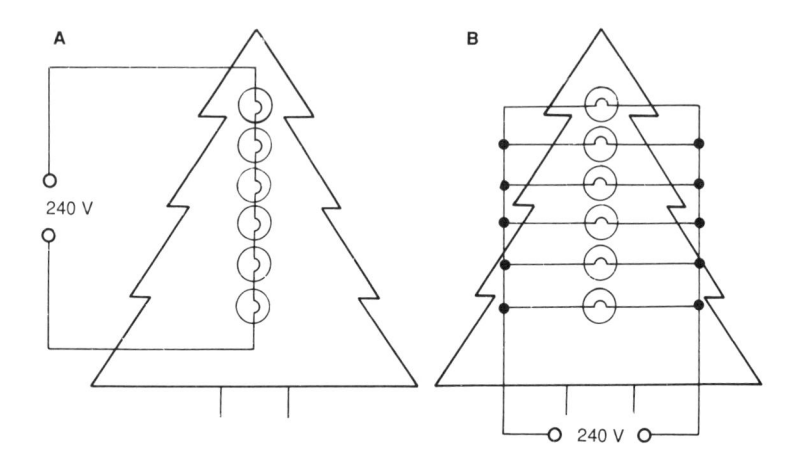

(i) After a while one bulb in each tree blows.
   (a) What happens to Family A's lights?
   (b) What happens to Family B's lights?
   (c) With each set of lights there is a spare bulb. Explain clearly what each family must do to find and replace their faulty bulb.
(ii) Each of Family A's bulbs has 10 W written on it whilst those of Family B have 20 W on them.
   (a) Whose bulbs are brightest? Explain your answer.
   (b) What is the voltage across each of the bulbs on
      (1) Family A's tree?
      (2) Family B's tree?
   (c) What is the current flowing through each of the bulbs on
      (1) Family A's tree?
      (2) Family B's tree?
   (d) Would a 13 ampere fuse be suitable for either of these circuits? Explain your answer.
(iii) Lighting circuits like these frequently don't have an earth wire. They use two-core electric wire. Both families are confident that they have wired their plugs correctly!! Can you see any faults in the diagrams on page 147?

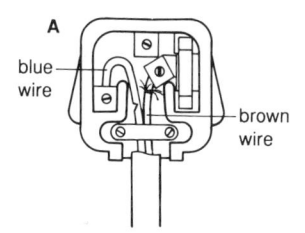

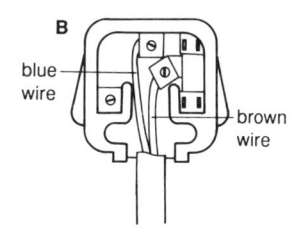

2 (i) What is the principal energy transformation which takes place when a 2 kW, 240 V, two bar electric fire is turned on?
  (ii) What is the power rating of the fire? Write a sentence explaining exactly what your answer means.
  (iii) To which part of the electric fire is the earth wire always connected? Explain what might happen if the fire became faulty and there was no earth wire.
  (iv) Where should the switch for turning the fire on and off be positioned? Explain your answer.
  (v) From the figures given in (i) calculate the current flowing through the fire.
  (vi) What is the most appropriate fuse for this circuit?
  (vii) Why would it be dangerous to connect two fires like the one described above to the same socket in a ring main?
  (viii) If any electrical appliance is found to be faulty when it is switched on, what is the first thing you must do?

3 The diagram on page 134 shows the route followed by domestic electricity in this country.
  (i) What device manufactures our electrical energy at a power station? Name three fuels which could be used to power this machine. State the principal energy transformation which takes place.
  (ii) Why is the electricity transmitted at high voltage?
  (iii) Suggest one reason why the power lines are suspended high above the ground on pylons.
  (iv) What happens to the electricity before it enters our homes? In just one sentence explain how this is done.
  (v) Why is alternating current transmitted rather than direct current?
  (vi) A transformer has 10 000 turns on its primary coil and 500 turns on its secondary. If a p.d. of 240 V a.c. is applied across the primary coil, calculate the output voltage across the secondary. Used in this way, this is a .... transformer.

ELECTRONICS
7.1 Controlling and using electrons

Radios, videos, hi-fis, etc, all contain electronic components. These control and manipulate the movement of electrons in a way which is useful to us.

Two important pieces of electrical equipment which demonstrate this are the cathode ray oscilloscope and the television.

The cathode ray oscilloscope (CRO)

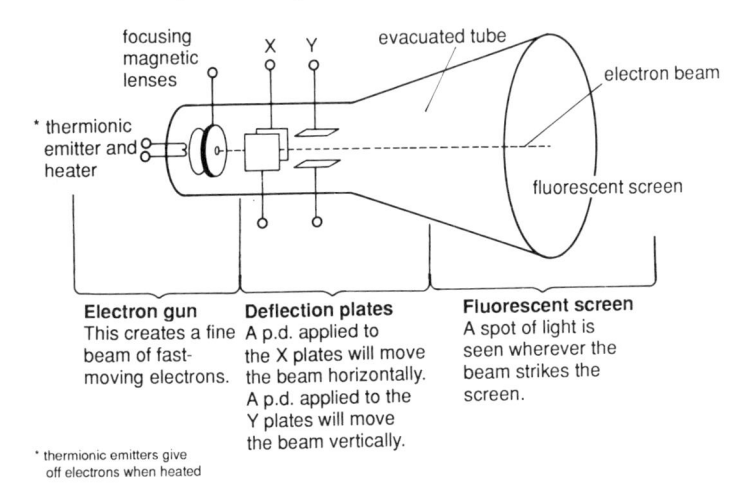

focusing magnetic lenses
X Y
evacuated tube
electron beam
* thermionic emitter and heater
fluorescent screen

Electron gun
This creates a fine beam of fast-moving electrons.

Deflection plates
A p.d. applied to the X plates will move the beam horizontally. A p.d. applied to the Y plates will move the beam vertically.

Fluorescent screen
A spot of light is seen wherever the beam strikes the screen.

* thermionic emitters give off electrons when heated

Screen displays

(i) No p.d. is being applied to either set of plates – the electron beam therefore hits the centre of the screen.

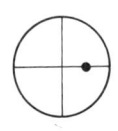

(ii) A p.d. is being applied to the X plates.

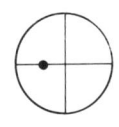

(iii) The reverse p.d. to (ii) is being applied to the X plates.

(iv) A p.d. is being applied to the Y plates.

The amount by which the spot is deflected is an indication of the size of the applied p.d., i.e. the CRO can be used as a voltmeter.

Timebase or sweep

The X plates have a circuit connected to them which can sweep the electron beam across the screen in a precise period of time. At low sweep frequencies a spot can be seen sweeping across the screen but at higher frequencies, because of persistence of the spots on the screen, a continuous horizontal line is seen.

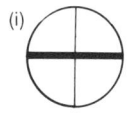

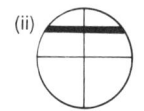

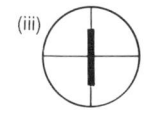

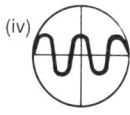

(i) The timebase is turned on but there is no p.d. applied to the Y plates. A horizontal line is seen across the centre of the screen.

(ii) The timebase is on and a p.d. is applied to the Y plates.

(iii) The timebase is off and an alternating p.d. is applied to the Y plates.

(iv) The timebase is on and an alternating p.d. is applied to the Y plates.

The television

Like the CRO, a television set generates an electron beam which is directed onto a screen. This beam sweeps very rapidly across and down the screen creating pictures in accordance with the signals the TV receives via its aerial.

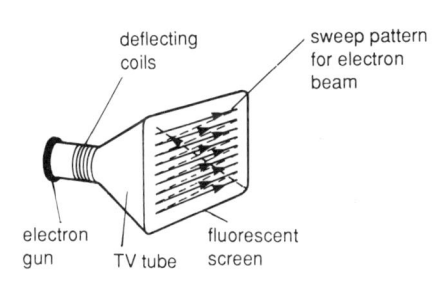

Colour televisions contain three separate electron guns. These produce a pattern of red, green and blue spots which combine to produce the coloured picture.

ELECTRONICS
7.2 Semiconductors

Materials such as copper which are good conductors of electricity contain lots of free charge carriers (e.g. electrons). Materials such as plastics are insulators because they contain no free charge carriers. Between these two extremes there is a third type of materials called semiconductors. Examples are silicon and germanium.

Semiconductor devices

1 The thermistor

A thermistor is a temperature sensitive resistor. As it becomes warm the thermal vibration of the lattice frees more charge carriers so reducing its resistance. Thermistors are often used in temperature sensing circuits such as fire alarms or thermostats.

2 Light dependent resistor (LDR)

An LDR is a light sensitive resistor. When light is shone onto an LDR its resistance drops. This happens because the incident light frees more charge carriers. An LDR is therefore an extremely useful light sensing device and is often used in burglar alarms, automatic lighting controls, etc.

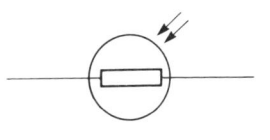

3 The junction diode

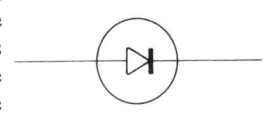

Although charges can flow through silicon and germanium their conductivities can be greatly improved by adding small amounts of impurities. If the impurity increases the number of negative charge carriers the material is known as an **n-type** semiconductor. If the impurity increases the number of positive charge carriers, the mate- rial is known as a **p-type** semiconductor.

A junction diode consists of a single crystal of silicon or germanium which has been 'doped' (impurities added) such that it is half n-type semiconductor and half p-type.

A junction diode will allow current to pass through it in just one direction. Connected like this the diode conducts and is said to be forward biased.

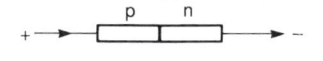

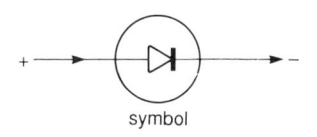

symbol

If the connections are reversed the diode is reverse biased and virtually no current passes through it.

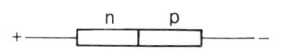

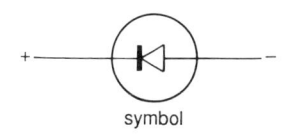

symbol

Because diodes conduct in only one direction, they can be used to change alternating current into direct current.

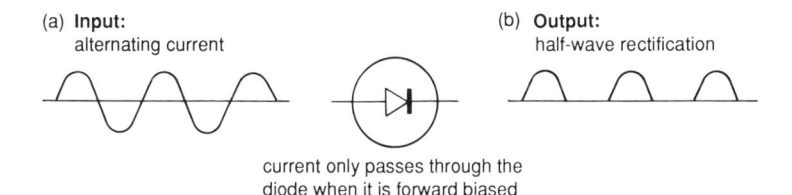

(a) **Input:**
    alternating current

(b) **Output:**
    half-wave rectification

current only passes through the diode when it is forward biased

If a fully rectified output is required, a bridge circuit containing four diodes may be used. When two of the diodes are forward biased the remaining two are reverse biased.

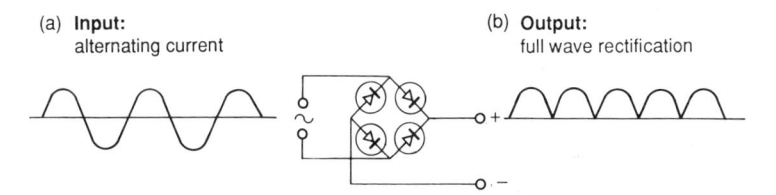

(a) **Input:**
    alternating current

(b) **Output:**
    full wave rectification

152 *Electronics*

4 Light emitting diode (LED)

An LED is a special type of junction diode which emits light when it is forward biased.

LEDs are often used as indicator lights to show if a piece of electrical equipment is switched on or to indicate the recording level of a tape recorder, etc. LEDs convert very little energy, and so are more economical (and more durable) than small bulbs for these purposes.

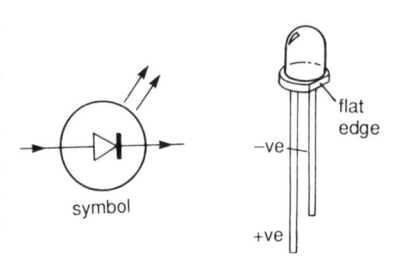

5 The transistor

If a crystal of silicon is doped to form a sandwich of n and p-type semiconductor, the component formed is called a transistor.

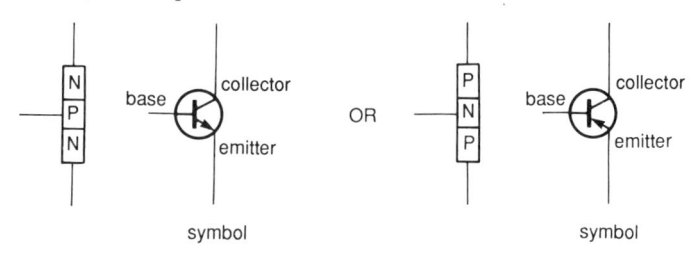

One use of a transistor is as an electronic switch. If there is no current in the base circuit, no charge is allowed to flow between the collector and the emitter, i.e. the collector/emitter current is turned on if the base voltage is high and off if it is low.

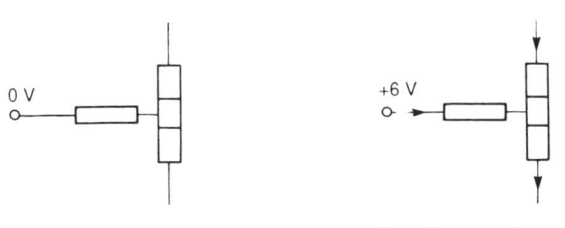

Transistor switch off   Transistor switch on

Uses of the transistor switch

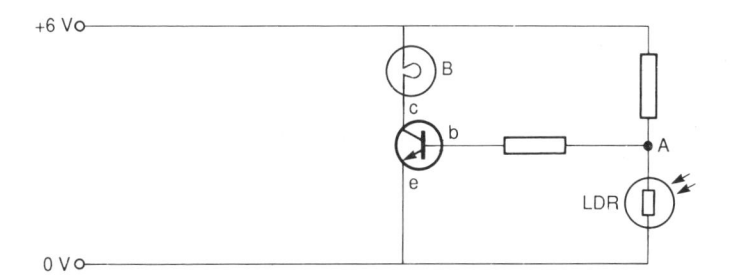

If no light falls on the LDR its resistance is high. The voltage at A is therefore high and the transistor is turned on. The bulb B therefore glows.

If light falls on the LDR the voltage at A falls. The transistor is therefore turned off and the bulb B ceases to glow.

A simple circuit such as this could be used to automatically turn on street lights as it becomes dark. If a thermistor were introduced into the circuit rather than an LDR, temperature rather than light would switch the transistor on and off.

Integrated circuits

In many modern electronic devices large numbers of transistors, resistors, diodes, etc., are replaced by a single component called an integrated circuit (commonly known as a silicon chip). These circuits are small, reliable and relatively cheap to manufacture.

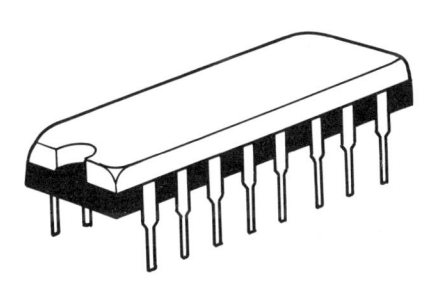

A single integrated circuit may contain the equivalent of up to 1 000 000 transistors, resistors etc.

ELECTRONICS
7.3 Electronic systems and gates

7

To operate a television or tape recorder it is not necessary to understand the workings of all the electrical components it contains. It is only necessary to know that by fulfilling certain conditions, e.g. pressing a switch, turning a knob, etc., a particular result will be obtained – the picture will be brighter, the sound will be louder, or the radio will receive the desired station. This 'black box' treatment of circuits is called the systems approach. For example, the amplification system used by pop groups:

microphone → amplifier → loudspeaker

Type	Symbol	Simple gate circuit
AND		
OR		
NOT		
NAND		
NOR		

Electronics

Many systems contain circuits which control the flow of information or current. They are known as **logic gates** because they only allow the information to pass if a set of conditions is fulfilled. The table below summarises the different types of gates and the conditions necessary for them to open.

We use truth tables to summarise in a simple way the results of all the possible combinations of inputs.

Input 0 – there is no input, no current, low voltage.
Input 1 – there is an input, current passes, high voltage, etc.

Circuit operation	Truth table			Gate operation
If current passes through X AND Y, the bulb L lights up.	Input X	Input Y	Output	There is an output if there is an input in both X AND Y.
	0	0	0	
	1	0	0	
	0	1	0	
	1	1	1	
If current passes through X OR Y, the bulb L lights up.	Input X	Input Y	Output	There is an output if there is an input from X OR Y or both.
	0	0	0	
	1	0	1	
	0	1	1	
	1	1	1	
If current passes through X bulb L does NOT light up. If current doesn't pass through X, bulb L does light.	Input	Output		The output is always opposite to the input i.e. if there is an input there is NOT an output.
	1	0		
	0	1		
If current passes through X AND Y bulb L does NOT light up.	Input X	Input Y	Output	There is NO output if there is an input in both X AND Y.
	0	0	1	
	0	1	1	
	1	0	1	
	1	1	0	
If current passes through X OR Y bulb L does NOT light up.	Input X	Input Y	Output	There is NO output if there is an input in X OR Y or both.
	0	0	1	
	0	1	0	
	1	0	0	
	1	1	0	

Uses of gates

Automatic street lights

To be effective, street lights need to be controlled by switches or gates which operate as the light level drops.

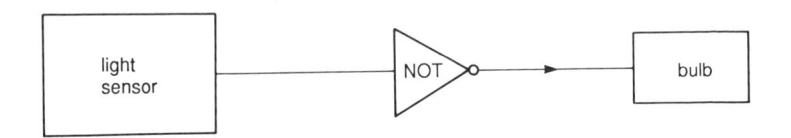

If light falls on the light sensor, there is an input to the NOT gate. There is therefore no output, i.e. the lamp is off.

If no light falls on the sensor, there is no input to the NOT gate. There is, therefore, an output, i.e. the lamp is on.

Thermostat indicator light

Many electrical appliances such as deep fat frying pans, irons, etc, contain thermostats. The system below could be used to indicate the state of the thermostat, e.g. show if the oil in the chip pan is at the correct temperature.

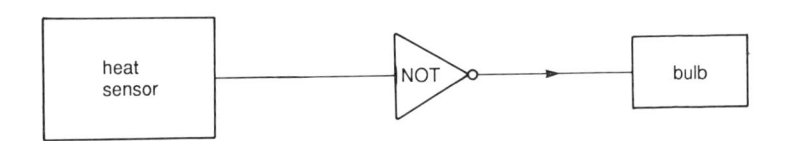

Q Whilst the chip fat is warming up the bulb is ....

Weather recorders

Many resorts quote weather statistics in their brochures in order to attract holidaymakers. The following two systems could be used to gather this information.

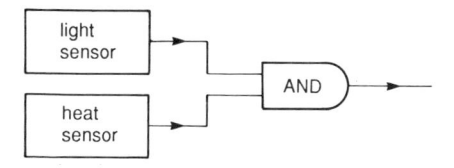

When the temperature is high AND it is daylight, there is an output from the AND gate, i.e. this system indicates when the temperature is above a certain level during the day.

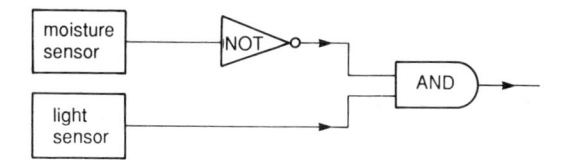

This system has an output when it is NOT raining during daylight hours.

Burglar alarm

There are many ways in which the presence of a burglar can be detected.

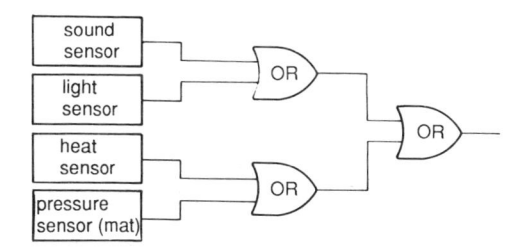

If none of these sensors detects the presence of an intruder, there is no output and the burglar alarm remains off. If any one of the sensors produces an output, the alarm will sound.

ATOMIC STRUCTURE AND RADIOACTIVITY
8.1 The Rutherford – Bohr atom

8

During the nineteenth century many ideas and theories were put forward as to the structure of an atom. The model which was eventually accepted was based on the work of two scientists: Ernest Rutherford in Britain and Niels Bohr in Denmark.

An atom consists of two parts:

1. a central part called the **nucleus** which contains small particles called **protons** and **neutrons**, and
2. an outer part which contains extremely small particles called **electrons** which orbit the nucleus at high speeds.

The electrons are negatively charged (1–) and have a mass just $\frac{1}{1836}$ of a proton or neutron.

The protons are positively charged (1+) and have a relative atomic mass of 1.

The neutrons are uncharged and also have a relative atomic mass of 1. (Because protons and neutrons are found in the nucleus they are often referred to as **nucleons**.)

Summary table

	Position	**Charge**	**Relative atomic mass**
Proton	in nucleus	1+	1
Neutron	in nucleus	0	1
Electron	outside nucleus	1–	$0 \left(\frac{1}{1836}\right)$

If an atom is neutral it must contain equal numbers of protons and electrons.

Since practically all the mass of an atom is contained in the nucleus its relative atomic mass must equal the number of protons and neutrons within its nucleus.

Using these ideas and the information contained in the **periodic table** it is possible to draw a picture of the atomic structure of different elements.

Atomic structure and the Periodic Table

The Periodic Table contains information about all known elements. It tells us an element's symbol, its mass number and its atomic number.

I	II						III	IV	V	VI	VII	0
				1 H Hydrogen 1								4 He Helium 2
7 Li Lithium 3	9 Be Beryllium 4						11 B Boron 5	12 C Carbon 6	14 N Nitrogen 7	16 O Oxygen 8	19 F Fluorine 9	20 Ne Neon 10
23 Na Sodium 11	24 Mg Magnesium 12						27 Al Aluminium 13	28 Si Silicon 14	31 P Phosphorus 15	32 S Sulphur 16	35·5 Cl Chlorine 17	40 Ar Argon 18
39 K Potassium 19	40 Ca Calcium 20	45 Sc Scandium 21	48 Ti Titanium 22	51 V Vanadium 23	52 Cr Chromium 24	55 Mn Manganese 25						

Consider the element helium. From the Periodic Table:

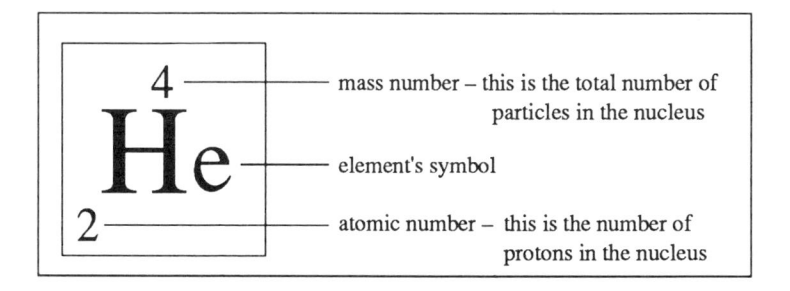

$^{4}_{2}$He

- 4 — mass number – this is the total number of particles in the nucleus
- He — element's symbol
- 2 — atomic number – this is the number of protons in the nucleus

Helium's atomic or proton number is 2, i.e. a helium nucleus contains 2 protons.

The atom is neutral, there must therefore be 2 orbiting electrons. Its mass (or nucleon) number is 4, i.e. the nucleus must also contain (4–2) neutrons.

The atomic structure of helium is therefore:

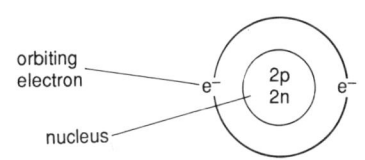

orbiting electron — e⁻ — 2p 2n — e⁻
nucleus

160 *Atomic structure and radioactivity*

Consider now the structure of a lithium atom. From the Periodic Table we can see that it has an atomic number of 3 and a mass number of 7. It should therefore contain 3 protons, 3 electrons and (7–3) neutrons.

Electrons travel around the nucleus of an atom in 'shells' or 'orbits' (rather like planets orbit the Sun.) Each orbit can only hold a certain number of electrons. When an orbit is full any remaining electrons must move into the next outer orbit.

The first orbit can hold 2 electrons. The second orbit can hold 8 electrons. The third orbit can hold 18 electrons.

The structure of a lithium atom is therefore:

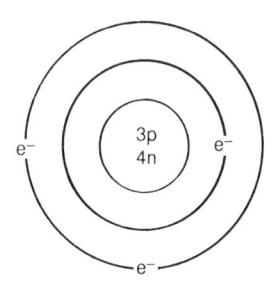

The structure of a sodium atom is therefore:

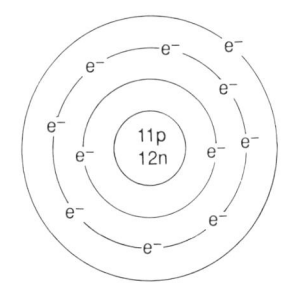

Isotopes

According to this model of the atom it is only possible to have whole number relative atomic masses, but if we look carefully at the Periodic Table on p. 159 we can see that this is not always true. Chlorine, for example, has an atomic number of 35.5 whilst its proton number is 17. A chlorine atom should therefore contain 17 electrons, 17 protons and (35.5–17) = 18.5 neutrons. But it is not possible to have half a neutron or half a proton, so how can chlorine have an atomic number of 35.5?

The problem was eventually solved when it was discovered that there were in fact two different kinds of chlorine atom. One contains 18 neutrons in its nucleus whilst the other contains 20. The mass number shown in the Periodic Table is an average of these two nuclei.

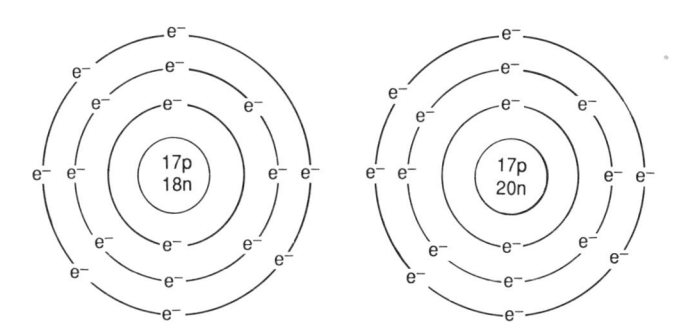

For example, if there were equal amounts of the two different chlorine atoms, we would expect the average to be

$$\frac{35 + 37}{2} = 36$$

However, in a normal sample of chlorine gas, three quarters of the atoms have a mass number of 35 whilst the remaining quarter have a mass number of 37. The average atomic number is therefore

$$\frac{35 + 35 + 35 + 37}{4} = 35.5$$

When a single element can have different numbers of neutrons in its nucleus, these different atoms are known as **isotopes**. Chlorine has two common isotopes – chlorine-35 and chlorine-37.

Many of the elements, especially the heavier elements, in the Periodic Table have isotopes which are unstable and decay, giving out **radioactive emissions**. These atoms are described as being radioactive isotopes, e.g. uranium-235, plutonium-239, radium-226.

ATOMIC STRUCTURE AND RADIOACTIVITY
8.2 Radioactivity

8

In 1896 a Frenchman named Henri Becquerel discovered that a uranium salt he was experimenting with was emitting some invisible rays which affected a photographic film. Although he did not know it at the time, he was in fact observing one of the effects of **radioactivity**.

Over the next few years several scientists studied these curious invisible rays, trying to discover all they could about them. Eventually they agreed that there were in fact three different kinds of radiation which could be emitted. These were called alpha (α) radiation, beta (β) radiation and gamma (γ) radiation.

Summary of the nature and properties of alpha, beta and gamma radiation

	α-radiation	β-radiation	γ-radiation
Nature	Helium nucleus ^4_2He	Fast moving electrons	Shortwave electromagnetic radiation
Charge	2+	1−	0
Mass	4	0	0
Penetrating power	Least penetrating. Stopped by several cm of air or sheet of paper.	More penetrating than α but less than γ. Stopped by several tens of cm of air or several mm of aluminium.	Most penetrating. Will travel through considerable thickness of lead.
Ionising* power	Very strongly ionising	Much less ionising than α but more than γ	Very little ionisation
Deflection by magnetic and electric fields	Small deflection	Very large deflection	No deflection
Detection by	Photographic film/cloud chamber/Geiger-Müller tube		

* When α, β or γ rays strike an atom they may **ionise** it, i.e. create an excess or shortage of electrons within the atom.

The diagram shown here illustrates the differing deflections the three types of radiation experience as they pass through a magnetic field. (Note the deflections are not to scale.)

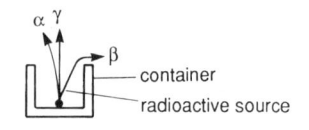

Cloud chamber

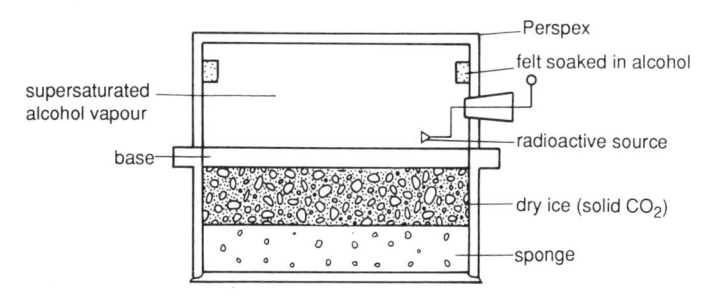

(Diagram of cloud chamber showing: Perspex, felt soaked in alcohol, supersaturated alcohol vapour, base, radioactive source, dry ice (solid CO_2), sponge)

The cloud chamber consists of a glass vessel containing alcohol vapour. The bottom of the chamber is kept cool by dry ice whilst the top is at room temperature. Because of this temperature difference there is in the chamber, just above the base, a 'supersaturated vapour' (as much vapour as possible 'dissolved' in the air but with no condensation present). If any radiation passes through the vessel it will ionise air molecules along its path, so creating ideal sites for the vapour to begin to condense. The result is a 'vapour trail' which indicates the path of the radioactive particles.

Alpha tracks These are usually straight, of equal length and quite thick (i.e. there has been considerable ionisation).

Alpha tracks

Beta tracks These are not straight, are of unequal length and are quite thin, indicating considerably less ionisation than in the case of the alpha particles.

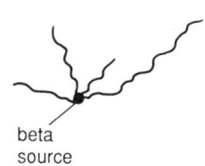

Beta tracks

Gamma tracks Although with care the vapour trails of gamma particles can be observed, under normal circumstances so little ionisation takes place that they are extremely difficult to see.

Where does radioactivity come from?

In 1903 two scientists, Rutherford and Soddy, suggested that the radiation must be coming from the very centre of the atom, i.e. the nucleus. Their reasoning was as follows:

α-radiation Most of the radioactive materials known at that time came from the same part of the Periodic Table. They were all very heavy elements with high proton and nucleon numbers. Perhaps the nucleus is unstable because too many protons and neutrons are packed closely together. In order to become more stable the nucleus needs to 'slim down a little', i.e. lose a little weight. One way in which the nucleus could achieve this would be to eject some protons and neutrons. It does this in the form of a helium nucleus, i.e. two protons and two neutrons bound together. This is called an **alpha particle.**

Radium decays to radon by α emission:

$$^{226}_{88}\text{Ra} \longrightarrow \,^{222}_{86}\text{Rn} + \,^{4}_{2}\text{He}$$

radioactive material   new slimmer nuclei   α-particle

β-radiation When β decay occurs, a neutron in the nucleus splits up to form a proton and an electron. This electron is emitted as a **beta particle** leaving an extra proton in the nucleus.

$$^{234}_{90}\text{Th} \longrightarrow \,^{234}_{91}\text{Pa} + \,^{0}_{1}\text{e}$$

β-particle

γ-radiation After an atom has emitted an alpha or beta particle, it may have an excess of energy which it has to get rid of. It does this by emitting a **gamma ray.**

By emitting a combination of alpha, beta and gamma radiation, atoms gradually change into new, lighter more stable elements.

Half-life

Some radioactive materials decay very rapidly, giving off a large number of particles in a short period of time. Others decay extremely slowly, their radiation being much less intense. We describe the rate of decay of a material by using the term **half-life**.

For example, suppose we begin with a thousand million atoms of an element X and then discover that after one minute half of these atoms have decayed leaving 500 million unaltered atoms. After a further minute, we would then find that only 250 million of the original atoms remain undecayed. From this we can see that the half-life of element X is one minute.

The half-life of a radioactive element is the time taken for half of its atoms to decay. For example:

Element	Half-life
Uranium	4.5×10^9 years (4 500 000 000)
Radium	1620 years
Radon	4 days
Polonium	3 minutes

If we plot a graph of the number of undecayed atoms against time for any radioactive element it would have the same shape as the graph shown on the left.

Radioactive decay is a completely *random* process. It is impossible to predict precisely when an atom is going to decay; it is only possible to predict how many atoms are going to decay over a period of time.

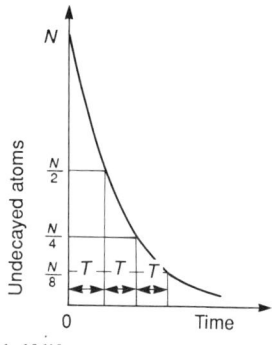

T = half-life

Radioactive isotopes and their uses

Some elements if they are bombarded with alpha or beta rays, become radioactive themselves. These new materials are called **radio-isotopes**, and can be very useful.

1 Tracers

If a radio-isotope is introduced into a patient's body, the progress of that element through the body can be observed using a Geiger-Müller tube. In this way the workings of various parts of the body can be checked, e.g. blood flow. Similarly, if a radio-isotope is introduced into a fertiliser, its efficiency can be determined by noting how quickly the isotope is taken up by the plants.

2 Medical treatment of cancer

Cobalt-60 is a radioactive isotope which emits powerful gamma rays. These can be used to treat various kinds of cancer.

3 Sterilising

Gamma rays from a suitable radio-isotope can be used to kill germs on surgical instruments, i.e. sterilise medical equipment.

4 Food preservation

Food goes bad and begins to rot because of the presence of microbes or germs. If food is irradiated with gamma rays these germs are killed and the food can be stored for a much longer period of time.

5 Carbon dating

All living things have inside them the naturally occurring radio-isotope carbon-14. When they die, the amount of carbon-14 in their bodies begins to decrease because of radioactive decay. By measuring the radioactivity of carbon-14 in, for example, a piece of wood or cloth or the body of an animal, it is possible to determine its age.

ATOMIC STRUCTURE AND RADIOACTIVITY
8.3 Nuclear power

8

Under certain circumstances, it is possible to make a stable atom unstable by pushing extra neutrons into its nucleus. If the nucleus becomes very unstable, rather than just emitting alpha, beta or gamma rays it may completely break apart. This process of an unstable nucleus breaking into several nuclei is called **fission** and is the basis of the nuclear bomb and the energy source of nuclear power stations.

If a neutron is shot into the nucleus of a uranium-235 atom, it becomes unstable and breaks apart, producing two new lighter elements, some fast-moving neutrons and a lot of energy.

$$^{235}_{92}U + ^{1}_{0}n \longrightarrow ^{236}_{92}U \longrightarrow 2 \text{ new elements} + 3\ ^{1}_{0}n + \text{energy}$$

If these neutrons now strike more uranium atoms, these too will split and so the chain reaction continues. If this continues uncontrolled, too much energy is released too quickly and an explosion results – a nuclear explosion.

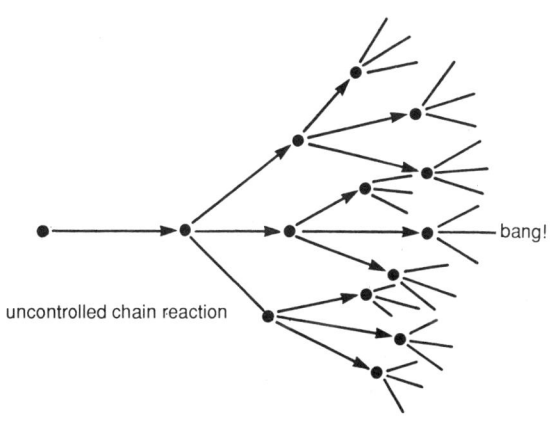

uncontrolled chain reaction — bang!

The energy produced by the uranium-235 when it splits is incredibly large and is of tremendous use when the chain reaction is controlled. In a nuclear power station, the rate at which the energy is released is controlled using boron rods. These absorb approximately two out of every three neutrons produced in the reaction. The chain reaction therefore neither runs away nor dies off, but just 'ticks over'.

Fusion

Most of our energy on Earth comes from the Sun. It too is produced by a nuclear reaction but not by fission. Instead it produces its energy when lighter atoms, e.g. isotopes of hydrogen, join together to produce heavier atoms. This process is called **fusion**.

$$^{2}_{1}H + {}^{2}_{1}H \longrightarrow {}^{3}_{2}He + {}^{1}_{0}n + \text{energy}$$

Although we have been able to duplicate this process (in a hydrogen bomb) we have not as yet been able to produce a controlled reaction which would allow us to make constructive use of this process.

The dangers of radioactivity

All three types of radioactivity (alpha, beta and gamma) can cause serious illness if sources which emit them are not handled correctly. The following rules will help ensure that you are not affected by radioactive sources.

1. Do not touch or remove any radioactive source without authorisation.
2. Never hold a radioactive source in your fingers, always pick it up using forceps.
3. Never hold a radioactive source near anyone's eyes.
4. When the radioactive source is not in use place it in its container and replace the lid.

QUESTIONS
8.4 Atomic structure and radioactivity   8

1 The diagram below shows the core of a nuclear reactor. When an atom of uranium-235 absorbs a neutron it becomes unstable and splits to produce two smaller new elements, three fast-moving neutrons and a large amount of energy. These neutrons may then be absorbed by three more uranium atoms and so the process continues.

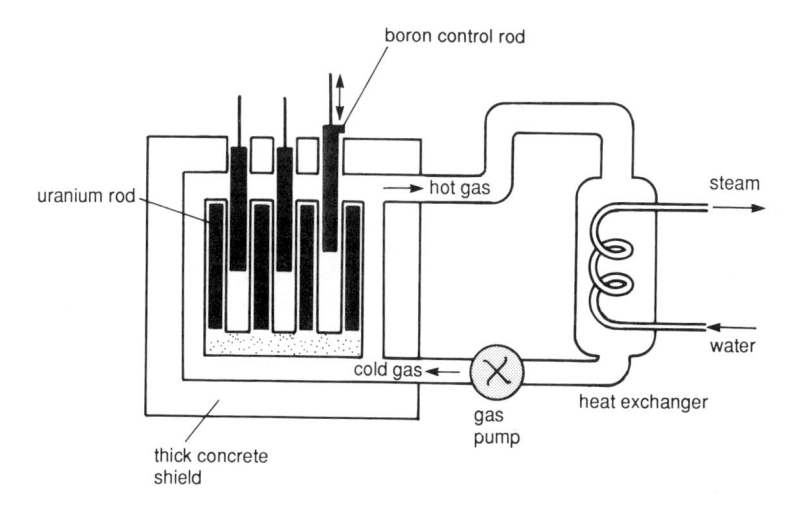

(i) Why is this process called a 'chain reaction'?
(ii) What would happen if the chain reaction were to proceed uncontrolled?
(iii) What happens as the control rods are pushed further into the nuclear pile?
(iv) What happens if the control rods are pushed in too far and are left there?
(v) What is the ideal position of the rods?
(vi) What happens to the energy produced by the nuclear reaction?
(vii) What happens in the heat exchanger?
(viii) What is the steam used for?
(ix) Why is the nuclear pile sealed in a thick concrete jacket?

170 *Atomic structure and radioactivity*

2 Today many liquids and gases are transported from place to place via underground pipelines. If, however, a pipe becomes faulty and leaks, the owners of the pipeline must be able to locate and fix the problem very rapidly. One way in which they could do this is by using a radioactive tracer which is added to the fluid in the pipe.
   (i) Give one advantage of putting a pipeline underground.
   (ii) Give three examples of the kinds of fluids which might be transported in this way.
   (iii) How would the pipeline inspector know when he had located a leak?
   (iv) What kind of radiation(s) should the tracer be emitting? Explain your answer.
   (v) Approximately how long a half-life should the tracer have? 1 second, 1 hour, 1 day, 1 year? Justify your answer.
   (vi) Suggest two other completely different situations where radioactive tracers might be used.

3 (i) What is the atomic number of element X?
   (ii) What is the mass number of element X?
   (iii) How many electrons in total does a neutral atom of element X have in its orbitals?
   (iv) How many electrons are there in the outer orbital of a neutral atom of element X?
   (v) Draw the nucleus of the new (neutral) element Y which is formed when element X emits an α-particle.

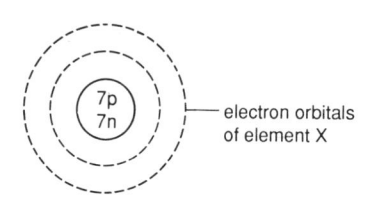

Element X

ANSWERS
1 Forces and motion

1. Speed = $\dfrac{\text{distance travelled}}{\text{time taken}} = \dfrac{500 \text{ m}}{20 \text{ s}} = 25 \text{ m/s}$

   This is an average speed, as no account is taken of any 'slowing down' or 'speeding up' during the 20 s.

2. Time taken = $\dfrac{\text{distance travelled}}{\text{speed}}$
   $= \dfrac{800 \text{ km}}{160 \text{ km/h}} = 5 \text{ h}$

3. Distance travelled = speed × time taken
   $= 180 \text{ km/h} \times 1\tfrac{1}{2} \text{ h}$
   $= 270 \text{ km}$

   Number of laps = $\dfrac{270 \text{ km}}{4.5 \text{ km}} = 60$

4. (i) OA – The bus starts from rest and accelerates uniformly.
   AB – The bus is moving at a constant speed.
   BC – The bus decelerates uniformly until it stops.
   CD – The bus is stationary.

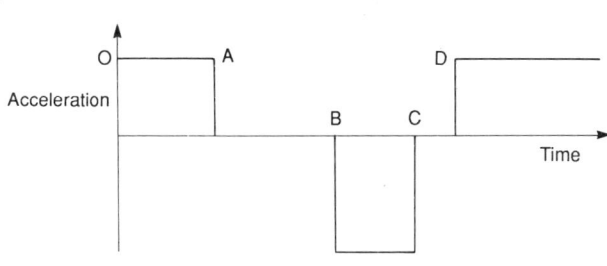

   (ii)

5 (i) $a = \dfrac{v-u}{t} = \dfrac{(200-0)\,\text{km/h}}{20\,\text{s}} = 10\,\text{km/h per second}$

This is the average acceleration, as the car's acceleration may have varied during this 10 s.

(ii) $a = \dfrac{v-u}{t} = \dfrac{(40-120)\,\text{km/h}}{20\,\text{s}} = -4\,\text{km/h per second}$

The deceleration of the train is 4 km/h per second
The acceleration of the train is −4 km/h per second

(iii) $a = \dfrac{v-u}{t} = \dfrac{(40-0)\,\text{km/h}}{4\,\text{s}} = 10\,\text{m/s}^2$

6 (i) At its highest point the stone is stationary, i.e. $v = 0$ m/s.

(ii) Using $\quad v = u + at$
$\quad\quad\quad\quad\quad 0 = u - 10\,\text{m/s}^2 \times 4\,\text{s}$
$\quad\quad\quad\quad \therefore u = 40\,\text{m/s}$

(iii) Using $\quad s = ut + \tfrac{1}{2}at^2$
$\quad\quad\quad\quad\quad s = 40\,\text{m/s} \times 4\,\text{s} + \tfrac{1}{2}(-10\,\text{m/s}^2) \times 16\,\text{s}^2$
$\quad\quad\quad\quad\quad\quad = 160\,\text{m} - 80\,\text{m}$
$\quad\quad\quad\quad\quad\quad = 80\,\text{m}$

(iv) Because the motion is symmetrical, the total time the stone is in the air is 8 s.

7 Using $\quad v^2 = u^2 + 2as$
$\quad\quad\quad\quad v^2 = 0 + 2 \times 5\,\text{m/s}^2 \times 90\,\text{m}$
$\quad\quad\quad\quad\quad = 900\,\text{m}^2/\text{s}^2$
$\quad\quad\quad\quad v = 30\,\text{m/s}$

This assumes the ski jumper starts from rest.
Using distance = speed × time
$\quad\quad\quad$ distance = 30 m/s × 3 s
$\quad\quad\quad\quad\quad\quad\quad = 90\,\text{m}$

8 Using $v = u + at$
$$v = 20 \text{ m/s} + 5 \text{ m/s}^2 \times 8 \text{ s}$$
$$= 60 \text{ m/s}$$

9 Four possible effects of force are
  (a) Changing the shape of an object, e.g. moulding clay.
  (b) Increasing the speed of an object, e.g. catapult.
  (c) Decreasing the speed of an object, e.g. catching a ball.
  (d) Changing the direction of a moving object, e.g. kicking a football

10 (i)

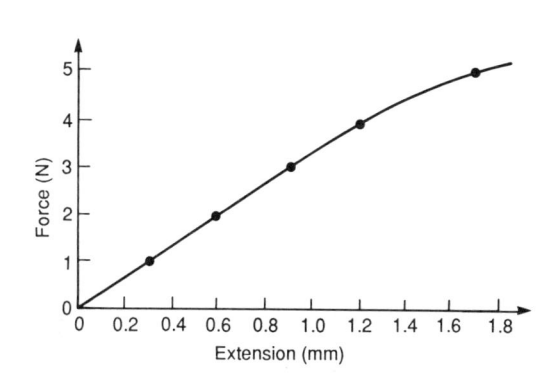

[Graph: Force (N) vs Extension (mm), showing a straight line from origin through (0.2, 1), (0.6, 2), (1.0, 3), (1.4, 4), curving to (1.8, 5)]

  (ii) Between 0 and 4 N the graph is a straight line graph through the origin, confirming Hooke's Law. However, beyond a force of 4 N the graph begins to curve, i.e. the limit of proportionality has been passed.
  (iii) The spring will contract uniformly, giving a permanent extension.

11 (i) $a = \dfrac{F}{m} = \dfrac{20 \text{ N}}{100 \text{ kg}} = 0.2 \text{ m/s}^2$

  (ii) $m = \dfrac{F}{a} = \dfrac{2 \text{ N}}{10 \text{ m/s}^2} = 0.2 \text{ kg or } 200 \text{ g}$

  (iii) $F = m \times a = 100\,000 \text{ kg} \times 2 \text{ m/s}^2$
  $= 200\,000 \text{ N}$

174 *Answers*

12 From the parallelogram of velocities the true velocity of the aircraft is 100.5 m/s 5.7° west of south.

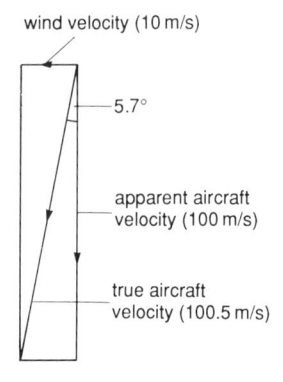

ANSWERS
2 Density and pressure

1 To find the density of cork:
  (a) Weigh the cork on the balance to find its mass.
  (b) Fill the eureka can with water.
  (c) Push the cork under the water using a needle.
  (d) Collect the water which is displaced and measure its volume. The volume of the displaced water is equal to the volume of the cork.
  (e) Calculate the density of the cork using the equation

  $$\text{density} = \frac{\text{mass}}{\text{volume}}$$

2 Density of aluminium = $\frac{5}{0.0018}$ 5/0.0018 kg/m³ = 2778 kg/m³

Density of steel = $\frac{15}{0.0019}$ 15/0.0019 kg/m³ = 7895 kg/m³

Density of lead = $\frac{100}{0.0090}$ 100/0.009 kg/m³ = 11 111 kg/m³

Answers 175

3 Pressure = $\frac{\text{force}}{\text{area}}$

  (i) $p = \frac{500 \text{ N}}{0.0025 \text{ m}^2} = 200\,000$ Pa

  (ii) $p = \frac{5000 \text{ N}}{0.1 \text{ m}^2} = 50\,000$ Pa

  (iii) $p = \frac{750 \text{ N}}{0.0125 \text{ m}^2} = 60\,000$ Pa

4 (i) The force applied to the drawing pin head is concentrated in a very small area at the pin's point. It is this high pressure which results in the pin penetrating the wood or cork.
  (ii) In this situation the high pressure at the point will result in the pin piercing the skin.

5 (i) Pressure in a liquid $= h \rho g$
    $= 20 \text{ m} \times 1000 \text{ kg/m}^3 \times 9.8 \text{ m/s}^2$
    $= 196\,000$ Pa

  (ii) If the swimmer had been diving in sea water he would have experienced a greater pressure, as the density of sea water is greater than that of fresh water.
  (iii) As the diver takes the balloon deeper, a greater pressure will be exerted upon it from all directions. The balloon will therefore become smaller (compressed) but will still be spherical.

6 At high altitudes the air is thin and its pressure is therefore very low. To prevent this lack of pressure affecting a pilot, he may wear a pressurised suit which keeps his body under a constant pressure of 1 atmosphere. (Pilots of civilian planes work in cabins which are pressurised to 1 atmosphere.)

7 (a) Each pupil in turns blows as hard as possible into the manometer.
  (b) The difference in the levels of the liquid in the two columns is noted.
  (c) The pupil who created the greatest difference in the level of the columns has the largest lung pressure.

ANSWERS
3 Work, energy and power

1. (i) Minimum force required to lift bucket = 500 N.

   (ii) Work done = force × distance moved
   = 500 N × 20 N
   = 10 000 J or 10 kJ

   (iii) As the tiles are lifted, electrical energy ⟶ gravitational potential energy.

   (iv) Power = $\dfrac{\text{work done}}{\text{time taken}} = \dfrac{10\,000\,\text{J}}{10\,\text{s}} = 1000$ W or 1 kW

   (v) If the winch is only 50% efficient only half of the input energy is used to do useful work. In this question the useful work done is 10 kJ. The energy input must therefore be 20 kJ (10 kJ useful and 10 kJ wasted).

   (vi) Friction in the winch would reduce the efficiency of the system. Also non-productive work has to be done in lifting the bucket containing the tiles.

   (vii) The efficiency of the system could be improved by
   (a) lubricating the winch to reduce friction,
   (b) using a lighter bucket.

2. (i) (a) Chemical energy from the food he has eaten.
   (b) Kinetic energy.
   (c) Gravitational potential energy.

   (ii) During the vault K. E. = gravitational P.E.

   $$\tfrac{1}{2}mv^2 = mgh$$
   $$\tfrac{1}{2}m \times 81\,\text{m}^2/\text{s}^2 = m \times 10\,\text{m/s}^2 \times h$$
   $$\therefore h = 4\,\text{m}$$

   (iii) K. E. = gravitational P. E.

   $$\tfrac{1}{2}mv^2 = mgh$$
   $$\tfrac{1}{2}m \times 100\,\text{m}^2/\text{s}^2 = m \times 10\,\text{m/s}^2 \times h$$
   $$\therefore h = 5\,\text{m}$$

(iv) Modern pole vaulters get extra energy by bending the pole (strain energy) and by using their leg and arm muscles during the actual vault.
(v) All the energy used in the vault is likely to end up as heat energy.

3 (i) Work done = force (weight) × distance moved
2×10^6 Nm = weight × 50 m
Weight of water = 40 000 N or 40 kN

(ii) (a) When the water has fallen 25 m it will have lost half its gravitational potential energy (2 MJ/2). This energy is transferred into kinetic energy, i.e. K.E. at 25 m = 1 MJ.
(b) When the water has lost all its gravitational potential energy, its K.E. = 2 MJ.

We have assumed that the system is 100% efficient.

(iii) If the generator is 40% efficient, 60% of the energy is lost,

i.e. $\frac{60}{100} \times 2$ MJ.

Therefore 1.2 MJ of energy is wasted.

(iv) There is less energy wasted if the electricity generated during the night can be used rather than stored. To encourage people to use night-time electricity, the Electricity Boards offer it at a cheaper price.

ANSWERS
4 Kinetic theory and heat

1 (i) The clothes dry as the water they contain gradually evaporates.
(ii) The ideal conditions for drying clothes are windy, hot and dry. Each of these conditions helps to speed up the rate of evaporation.

2 (a) The hot water heats the radiator by conduction.
(b) The air immediately next to the radiator becomes warm by conduction, less dense and therefore rises, i.e. a convection current is set up.

178 *Answers*

   (c) This convection current carries energy all around the room.
   (d) Some energy is radiated into the room (the amount depending upon the nature of the surface of the radiator).

(i) If the radiator was painted black more energy would be radiated into the room.

(ii) If silver foil was placed between the radiator and the wall, energy which would have warmed the wall would be reflected back into the room.

(iii) Most plastics are insulators. If a radiator was made out of plastic much of the energy would be prevented from heating the air around it.

(iv) If the radiator was fixed high up on a wall the convection current it sets up would only heat the top of the room.

A thermostatic valve automatically turns off the flow of hot water to the radiator when the room is at the required temperature. By working in this way it helps conserve energy.

3 (i) (a) Energy from the hot water will enter the hand.
      (b) Energy from the fresh meat will flow into the freezer.
      (c) The top of an oven is warmer than the bottom. Therefore, when the cake is moved higher, energy will flow into it making it hotter.

(ii) If scalding water is spilt on someone's hand, energy passes from the water to the hand as the water cools down. If, however, steam comes into contact with a hand it gives up its latent heat of vaporisation (in order to change into water) and then it gives up even more energy as it cools. Burns from steam are therefore much more serious than those from boiling water.

One way in which excess energy can be taken out of the skin is to immerse the burnt area in cold running water.

4 Using $H = m \times c \times (T_2 - T_1)$
$= 0.4 \,\text{kg} \times 4200 \,\text{J/(kg K)} \times (50 - 10)\,°C$
$= 67\,200 \,\text{J} \text{ or } 67.2 \,\text{kJ}$

5 (i) The dark coloured collector plate is a good absorber of the Sun's radiation. When it becomes warm, energy is transferred to the copper pipe.
 (ii) Copper is a good conductor of heat. The heat transfer from the collector plate through the pipe to the water is much more efficient if the pipe is made from a material which is a good conductor.
 (iii) The pipe zigzags back and forth because the greater the length of pipe in contact with the collector plate the better the heat transfer.
 (iv) The back of the collector plate is fixed to an insulator to prevent heat loss from the back of the panel. A suitable material for the insulator might be polystyrene, fibreglass, etc.
 (v) If the front of the panel is covered with glass energy is trapped inside the panel (as in a greenhouse).
 (vi) Double glazing would reduce any heat loss from the front of the panel, but it is expensive.

ANSWERS
5 Waves

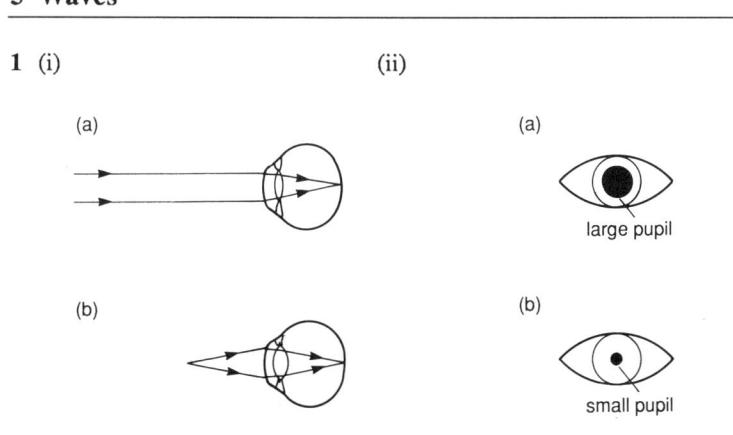

1 (i)   (ii)

(a)

(a) large pupil

(b)

(b) small pupil

 (iii) Explorers in the Arctic or Antarctic suffer from snowblindness because the snow-covered land reflects too much light through the pupil onto the retina of the eye. One way of avoiding this problem is to wear dark glasses.

180 Answers

(iv) Someone who suffers from shortsightedness should wear concave or diverging lenses when looking at distant objects, as these will diverge the rays a little, causing them to meet on the retina.

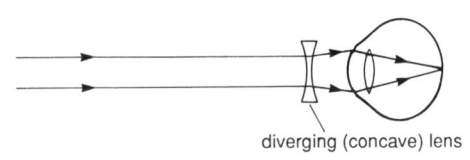

diverging (concave) lens

(v) Someone who suffers from longsightedness should wear convex or converging lenses when looking at near objects, as these will converge the rays a little, causing them to meet on the retina.

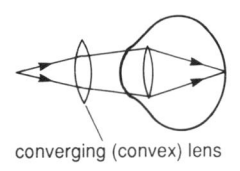

converging (convex) lens

2 (i) In a tailor's shop a plane mirror will be used, as this creates an upright image the same size as the object.
 (ii) A shaving or make-up mirror is concave, as this produces a magnified upright image.
 (iii) A convex mirror is often positioned on a sharp bend because it produces a diminished upright image from a wide field of vision.
 (iv) A dentist will use a concave mirror, as this will produce an upright magnified image of the patient's teeth.
 (v) The mirror used at the back of a searchlight is parabolic concave, as this produces a parallel beam of light.

3 When the driver of a car looks in his rear view mirror, he will see an image of the word the right way round and realise that there is an ambulance behind him.

4 A transverse wave is one which vibrates at right angles to the direction in which it is moving, e.g. light waves, water waves.

A longitudinal wave is one which vibrates along the direction in which it is moving, e.g. sound waves.

5 (i)

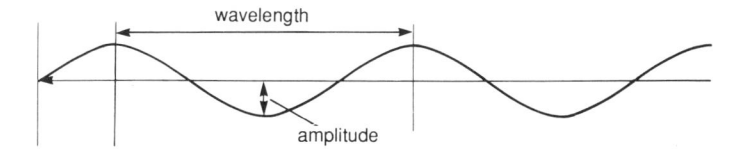

[diagram of a wave showing wavelength measured crest-to-crest and amplitude measured from axis to crest]

(ii) (a) If the wavelength became shorter the pitch of the note would increase.
(b) If the amplitude got larger the note would sound louder.
(c) If the shape of the wave changed the quality of the note would alter.

6 Using $v = f\lambda$,
$v = 250 \text{ Hz} \times 1.2 \text{ m}$
$\therefore v = 300 \text{ m/s}$

The speed of sound is 300 m/s.

7 (i) 'Supersonic' means faster than the speed of sound.
(ii) 'Ultrasonic' means that the frequency of the note is too high for the human ear to detect, i.e. people can't hear the note.
(iii) People who have to work with noisy machinery, e.g. tractors, often wear ear protectors.

8

Type of wave	X-rays	Ultraviolet	Visible light	Infra-red	Microwaves	Radio waves
Speed	3×10^8 m/s	3×10^8 m/s	3×10^8 m/s	3×10^8 m/s	3×10^8 m/s	3×10^8 m/s
Detection	photographic plate	fluorescent	eye	sense of feel or touch	heating effect (cooking)	radio receiver
Use	medical	Sun tan	seeing	cooking and photography	microwave oven	radio

182 *Answers*

(i) Wavelength.
(ii) Frequency.
(iii) Properties which are common to all the waves of the electromagnetic spectrum include reflection, refraction, diffraction, they all travel at the same speed in a vacuum, are all transverse waves and can all travel through a vacuum.

9 (i) The echo detector will hear the echo sooner than expected as the waves travel a much shorter distance before being reflected back up by the shoal of fish. The sooner the echo returns the nearer the shoal is swimming to the surface.
(ii) If the sea-bed is very uneven, e.g. the ship passes over an underwater hill or mountain, the time that elapses before the echo is heard will become shorter.
(iii) (a) 750 m

(b) Time $= \dfrac{\text{distance}}{\text{speed}}$

$= \dfrac{2 \times 250 \text{ m}}{1500 \text{ m/s}}$

$= \dfrac{1 \text{ s}}{3}$

∴ An echo will be heard after $\frac{1}{3}$ s.

ANSWERS
6 Electricity

---

1 (i) (a) All the bulbs go out (series circuit).
(b) Just the faulty bulb goes out (parallel circuit).
(c) Family A should:
1. **Turn off the supply** (240 V can be a lethal supply).
2. Replace one of the bulbs with the spare.
3. Turn the supply back on.
4. Repeat the steps 1, 2 and 3 until all the bulbs light up when supply is switched on.

Family B should:
1. Note which bulb is not glowing.
2. **Turn off the supply**.

3. Replace the faulty bulb.
4. Turn the supply back on.

(ii) (a) Family B's bulbs will be brighter. These have a higher peak rating and are therefore converting electrical energy into heat and light energy more quickly than Family A's lights.

(b) 1. 40 V, i.e. $\frac{240}{6}$ (series circuit).
2. 240 V, i.e. same as the supply (parallel circuit).

(c) 1. $P = V \times I$
$10 \text{W} = 40 \text{ V} \times I$
$I = 0.25 \text{ A}$

2. $P = V \times I$
$20 \text{W} = 240 \text{ V} \times I$
$I = 0.083 \text{ A}$

(d) No. A 13 A fuse is far too large. A 1 A or 3 A fuse would be much better as these would give the circuit more protection.

(iii) Faults with Family A's plug:
1. Neutral wire is cut.
2. Stray whiskers from live wire.
3. Inner wire clamped instead of outer cable.

Faults with Family B's plug:
1. The fuse has been omitted.
2. There is no wire connected to the neutral pin. It has been connected to the earth pin by mistake.
3. The clamp for the outer cable is missing.

2 (i) Electrical energy ⟶ heat and light energy.

(ii) The power rating of an electrical appliance is a statement of how rapidly an energy transformation is taking place, e.g. a 2 kW electric fire is transforming 2000 J of electrical energy into heat and light energy every second.

(iii) The earth wire is always connected to the metal outer casing of an electrical fire. If the heating element of an electrical fire broke and made contact with the outer casing there would be danger of electrocution if someone touched the fire (i.e. they become the earth connection).

184 *Answers*

(iv) All switches should be included in the *live* part of the circuit otherwise the appliance is not isolated, i.e. electrical energy can still enter.

(v) $$P = V \times I$$
$$2000 \text{ W} = 240 \text{ V} \times I$$
$$I = 8.3 \text{ A}$$

(vi) The most appropriate fuse for this fire is 13 A.

(vii) If two 2 kW fires are connected to the same socket there is a danger that the heating effect of the current 'drawn' by both fires could be sufficient to start an electrical fire (i.e. the current would be greater than 13 A).

(viii) **Turn the appliance off and unplug it.**

3 (i) Generators manufacture our electricity. Oil, coal, gas and nuclear fuel could be used in a power station.
Chemical energy ⟶ electrical energy.

(ii) There is less energy lost if the electrical energy is transmitted at high voltage and low current.

(iii) To avoid accidents (i.e. to stop people coming into contact with them).

(iv) The voltage is decreased before entering our homes. This is done by feeding the electrical energy into a step-down transformer.

(v) It is much easier (and wastes less energy) to change the currents and voltages of alternating electrical supplies as opposed to direct electrical supplies.

(vi) Using $$\frac{N_s}{N_p} = \frac{V_s}{V_p}$$

$$\frac{500}{10000} = \frac{V_s}{240 \text{ V}}$$

$$V_s = \frac{500 \times 240 \text{ V}}{10000}$$

$$= 12 \text{ V}$$

This is a step-down transformer.

ANSWERS
8 Atomic structure and radioactivity

1. (i) The process is called a chain reaction because as each atom of uranium-235 splits it releases neutrons which cause other uranium atoms to split and so on.
   (ii) If uncontrolled, the chain reaction would accelerate very rapidly and the rate of release of energy would be so high that there would be a danger of nuclear explosion.
   (iii) As the control rods are pushed further into the nuclear pile they absorb more of the neutrons and so slow down the chain reaction.
   (iv) If the control rods are pushed in too far too many neutrons are absorbed and the chain reaction begins to 'die'.
   (v) The ideal position for the control rods is reached when the reaction neither accelerates nor dies but just 'ticks over'.
   (vi) The heat energy produced by the nuclear reaction is used to heat gases which are pumped around the core.
   (vii) Inside the heat exchanger the gases give some of their energy to the water, so changing it into steam.
   (viii) The steam produced in the heat exchanger could be used to drive a steam turbine or generator which in turn will manufacture our electricity.
   (ix) The nuclear pile is sealed in a thick concrete jacket
      (a) to withstand the high pressure of the circulating gases and
      (b) to reduce the risk of workers being exposed to high levels of radiation.

2. (i) Pipelines are often put underground so as to avoid spoiling the environment.
   (ii) Fluids which might be transported by a pipeline include water, oil, coal gas, natural gas, etc.
   (iii) The pipeline inspector would know he had located the leak when his Geiger-Müller counter indicated an increase in count rate.
   (iv) The kind of radiation emitted by the tracer used would depend upon the nature of the pipe and how deep it was laid. However, it is most likely that a tracer which emits gamma radiation would be used, as a high penetrating power is needed to reach the surface.
   (v) For a short pipeline a half-life of one hour may be sufficient, but it is more likely that a tracer with a half-life of one day would be used. This would give sufficient time to find the leak before the level of radiation drops too low and yet does not leave large amounts of residual radiation well after the leak has been discovered and repaired.

(vi) Tracers can be used in the human body (e.g. bloodstream or digestive system) or in an engine (e.g. lubricating or cooling system).

3 (i) The atomic number of element X is 7 (7 protons).
 (ii) The mass number of element X is 14 (7 + 7).
 (iii) Element X will have 7 electrons orbiting its nucleus. (If the atom is neutral, number of neutrons = number of electrons.)
 (iv) There are two electrons in the inner orbital and five in outer orbital of a neutral atom of element X.

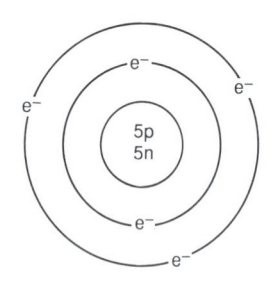

(v)

i.e. $\quad ^{14}_{7}X \quad \longrightarrow \quad ^{10}_{5}Y \quad + \quad ^{4}_{2}He$

$\qquad\qquad\qquad\qquad\qquad$ new atom $\quad$ α-particle